Spatial Patterning among Animal Bones in Settlement Archaeology

An English regional exploration

Bob Wilson

TEMPVS REPARATVM

BAR British Series 251
1996

British Archaeological Reports are published by

Tempvs Reparatvm
Archaeological and Historical Associates Limited
29 Beaumont Street
Oxford OX1 2NP

BAR 251

Spatial Patterning among Animal Bones in Settlement Archaeology: An English regional exploration

Tempvs Reparatvm Volume Editor: Rajka Makjanić

Printed in England by The Basingstoke Press

ISBN 0 86054 840 6

All BAR titles available from:

Hadrian Books Ltd
122 Banbury Road
Oxford OX2 7BP
England

The current BAR catalogue with details of all titles in print, prices and means of payment, is available free from Hadrian Books

All volumes are distributed by Hadrian Books Ltd

To Murray Neal Wilson
1968–1991

ABSTRACT

A recent field of scientific discovery deals with the spatial patterning of bones and other artefacts at human settlements. Consistencies and differences of bone patterning can be found at archaeological sites dating from ancient hominid occupation floors to the immense and complex stratigraphy of modern towns and cities. Excavations from the Upper Thames Valley, England, are used to illustrate the development of methods and findings by one biologist, particularly the central and peripheral distribution of coarse and fine bone debris at sites. A cross cultural and multiperiod model of descriptive, interpretive and explanatory ideas is put forward and brings in natural activities such as scavenging and detritus clearance, and cultural activities such as butchery, industrial and ritual processes.

CONTENTS

LIST OF FIGURES

LIST OF TABLES

PREFACE

By the Director of the Oxford Archaeological Unit

Bob Wilson's book is about bones; it is partly the personal history of a bone archaeologist.

The early 1970's saw a significant expansion of field archaeology in Britain. Many young, inexperienced and optimistic archaeologists suddenly had the opportunity to indulge in their fascination for the past. In Oxford we attempted to exploit the possibilities of rescue archaeology to carry out explicitly regional research.

The reconstruction of past economies was in fashion. This was a task which required biologists. At the Oxford Archaeological Unit we were fortunate to recruit three natural historians – Martin Jones, who worked on carbonized plants; Mark Robinson, who specialised in waterlogged plants and insects; and Bob Wilson, a bone specialist.

Prior to the 1970's, if archaeologists recovered biological data at all, the result was often a rather sterile species list. Palaeobotanists and zoologists were either remote boffins in the lab or self-taught archaeologists. The mid 70's in the OAU was a challenging period when field archaeologists and biologists worked closely together, constructing mutual research agendas. It also was a time when optimistic youth discovered that archaeology was not easy. The remains of the past were fragile, messy and often opaque. But the sites were exciting and varied. Almost for the first time in British archaeology we could work on a large scale, develop systems to sample and compare sites, and gather data on a sufficient scale to answer questions and pose new ones.

In particular we rapidly came to realise that the fragments of the past did not speak for themselves. The archaeological record itself had to be understood before history could be written. Bob Wilson's book conveys a sense of that learning process.

It is also a book of ideas based on years of practice. Too often specialists operate at a distance from the front line. And those who are there rarely have time to reflect. An unfortunate illness removed Bob Wilson from the hurly-burly. This was a loss to his colleagues in the field, but as a result Bob gained time for reflection. Time to express his thoughts in a book aimed not only at his fellow bone specialists, but at all thinking field archaeologists. What follows is that book.

David Miles

16 October 1995

GENERAL SPATIAL CONSIDERATIONS AND THEIR BACKGROUND

Prologue

Human activity and organisation occupy space. So do the remnants of human occupation. For the archaeologist, the spatial pattern of human occupation ought to be separated, first into the documentation of the distribution of material remains, and second, into the study of the ecological and cultural processes by which settlements formed, operated, developed and, eventually, disintegrated.

Spatial ordering and coherence of archaeological remains is diversely evident in the forms of the ruins of Stonehenge and the earthworks of medieval castles. It may be observed in the crop markings of circular Bronze Age ditches and contrasted with the frequently rectilinear and extensive layout of excavated Roman rural and urban settlements. Less apparent, but equally important, is the spatial patterning of potsherds, bones and other detritus throughout the earthen deposits that fill ancient field and farmyard ditches, storage pits, wells, floor levels and external layers of long–demolished domestic buildings, shrines, factories and other elaborate structures. For, in the pattern of remains contained within the soil is imprinted vital information on how our forebears interacted spatially with the natural world.

Aim

The purpose of this book to describe and substantially explain the spatial configurations of animal bones and other site debris in archaeological deposits as shown by excavations and experimental studies, mainly in the Upper Thames Valley, England. Demonstrating this is felt to be so fundamental to archaeology yet so little deliberated over by some investigators that one may ask when regional and national investigations of bone distributions will rest on a secure scientific and other methodological basis for the first time?

Acknowledgements

The excavation teamwork that underlies the bone analysis presented in this volume has been acknowledged in part elsewhere before now but it is important to reemphasise the planning foresight and effort that the Oxford Archaeological Unit put in under its former director Tom Hassall. Mike Parrington, David Miles, Mark Robinson, Tim Allen, Philip Page and George Lambrick directed the major informative excavations with Mark Robinson and Martin Jones helping to supply planning and methodological expertise. Brian Durham, Simon Palmer, Claire Halpin, Richard Chambers, Maureen Mellor, Diane Hofdahl and Gwyne Oakley played significant parts in the functioning of the Unit during excavation and post excavation work. Bruce Levitan took up the bone work where I left off. John Musty and Brian Davison (Department of the Environment), Clifford Price and Tony Fleming (English Heritage), Barry Cunliffe (Institute of Archaeology, Oxford), and Roger Hobby (University Museum, Oxford) aided the post–excavation work by their administration. Financing of the bone work came through a variety of funding, chiefly through Amey Roadstone Corporation and later the Ancient Monuments Laboratory, London. To all these colleagues and institutions and many others playing smaller roles a considerable debt is owed. Without their contributions our regional knowledge of spatial patterning would exist only in a rudimentary form.

I am very grateful to Tim Allen, Sebastian Payne, Terry O'Connor, Bill Toner and David Miles for their willingness, knowledge and patience which were applied to read and comment on the text. Roger Thomas and Chris Balkwill also assisted in this. I am indebted too to Michael Schiffer, who supplied me with photocopying of relevant American literature, and to Sebastian Payne for keeping me in touch with developments elsewhere.

In this book chapters 2, 3, 6, 9–11, and 14–17 are largely original texts. Chapter 1 is a greatly expanded version of Wilson 1994 (copyright Oxbow Books), chapters 4 and 5 are drawn mainly from Wilson 1993 (copyright Oxford Archaeological Unit), chapters 7 and 8 from Wilson 1989a (copyright La Pensee Sauvage, Editions) and unpublished b, chapter 12 from part of Wilson 1989a (copyright La Pensee Sauvage, Editions), and chapter 13 partly from Wilson 1994 (Oxbow Books). Grateful thanks go to the above organisations for permission to publish from the previously presented works.

Permission to publish additional quotes has been given by the following: Catherine Bell, Hans Peter Blankholm, David Brown, Christopher Carr, Clive Gamble, Ian Hodder (on behalf of David Clarke), R. Lee Lyman, David Miles, H. L. Moore, Sebastian Payne, Keith Wade, Robert Whallon, and John E. Yellen.

Permission to publish two figures has been given by: Lewis R. Binford (Fig.61 from In pursuit of the past (1983), London: Thames and Hudson; Betty J. Meggers (Fig. 86 from Hesse and Wapnish 1985, Animal bone archaeology: from objectives to analysis, Washington: Taraxacum Press). Thanks also go to David Miles for allowing figures to be taken from the publications of the Oxford Archaeological Unit.

PART I

GENERAL SPATIAL CONSIDERATIONS AND THEIR BACKGROUND

Further more, the information obtained about any lateral variation may itself be of the greatest interest (Payne 1972a, 66).

Spatial patterns among artifacts over archaeological sites can be very important to the archaeologist. They can be used not only in traditional ways to reconstruct the activity areas, toolkits and lifeways of past peoples, but also to formulate and test hypotheses on the state and organisation of past cultural systems and natural environmental systems (Carr 1985, 302).

......it is argued that most intrasite spatial investigations in Scandinavia and North West Europe have fallen short of coming to grips with a number of important issues of intrasite spatial analytical research (Blankholm 1991, 23).

Chapter 1

Spatial Patterning of Animal Bones and the Literature

It is neither especially pertinent nor feasible to review in detail the full national and global literature on spatial analysis of sites and artefacts, particularly in the spatial relationships between sites or **intersite analysis**. Relevant literature is extensive on the latter but much is unrewarding to the purpose of this book which is devoted to the understanding of **intrasite archaeology**; in particular, to the study of the spatial relationships among bones at individual settlements in Britain.

Despite the evasion of reviewing the general literature of spatial analysis, one of the first and pivotal contributions to the theory of spatial relationships at European sites is the work of David Clarke in Spatial archaeology and published in 1977. Quotations demonstrate his influence on archaeological thinking:–

> The main claim will be that the retrieval of archaeological information from various kinds of spatial relationship is a central aspect of the international discipline of archaeology....' (Clarke 1977, 1).

> 'Spatial archaeology might be defined – as the retrieval of information from archaeological spatial relationships and the study of the spatial consequences of former hominid activity patterns within and between features and structures and their articulation within sites, site systems and their environments: the study of the flow and integration of activities within and between structures, sites and resource spaces from the micro [personal and social space], to the semi–micro [communal space] and macro [geographic and economic space] scales of aggregation.' (1977, 9–11).

> ....the aim of this study is the search for and explanation of spatial patterns and singularities in the form and function of the particular patterns of allocation [human choice processes] in order to gain fuller understanding of the adaptive role of particular systems at work and a better knowledge of the underlying causality of analytic spatial variability in general.' (1977, 10).

> 'We are certainly only just beginning to explore the possibilities of archaeological spatial theory at sufficient level of generality to make it [a] cross cultural, cross time and cross specialisation [sic] to the degree necessary for a respectable international set of disciplinary theory.' (1977, 28).

Clarke thus drew attention to important overall strategies, practical requirements and problematical outcomes of archaeological investigations, particularly in this country. He highlighted deficiencies of archaeological teaching during the 1960's and 1970's.

Despite the growing awareness and contribution of contemporary and subsequent authors and editors to the development of spatial studies in general archaeological theory (Hodder & Orton 1976, Hodder 1978, Hietala 1984a, Carr 1984 and 1985, Allen, Green & Zubrow 1990, Kent 1990, Malina & Vasicek 1990, Blankholm 1991, Ardener 1993, Fotheringham & Rogerson 1994, and Parker Pearson & Richards 1994), the application of principles of relevance to bone studies has been limited and neglected by many investigators, the leading exception being Lewis Binford (1978 and 1983). Nevertheless, soon after the publication of Spatial archaeology, the relevance of the work of Clarke to bone specialists was well set out by Clive Gamble (1978) within the context of the development of British sampling theory:–

> 'Sites are the result of past human activity and as such must be expected to display differentiation with regard to the types of activity carried out, their intensity and location within a defined area. The spatial patterning of activity within bounded limits is common to societies ranging in scale from hunter–gatherers to complex urban activities. Human action has spatial consequences and this has implications for the patterning of archaeological material in contexts.' (Gamble 1978, 330).

> 'The population we are sampling as bone analysts is space and the sampling units within the sampling frame are contexts and features.' (1978, 338).

> 'Although studied as an independent population, bones must eventually be integrated into the spatial context from which they were first drawn.... They must contribute to our appreciation of variability and its causes in the archaeological record.' (1978, 347).

Noticeably, Gamble could draw on scarcely any British findings from spatial studies. The principle of placing bones in spatial contexts was supported by limited evidence of variable species representation in different types of feature – for example, the study of Richard Meadow (1975) of deposits inside and out of the foundations of former buildings at Hajji Firuz, Turkey, and the work of Hans–Peter Uerpmann (1976) on bones in the Roman pits at Dangstetten, Germany. In the case of Meadow the proposition that such distributions could be seen primarily as spatial patterns was an inference rather than a demonstration. Gamble's paper also included references to scavenging and other relevant processes by Glynn Isaac (1967) and C. K. Brain (1967) – studies farther afield in Africa – but to no comparable study in Britain although spatial ramifications of scavenging had been noted (Wilson 1975, 120). The argument might have been strengthened by mention of further studies of spatial patterning at !Kung camps in Botswana by John Yellen

(1977), a metrical study of bone spacing at Olduvai Gorge by Milla Ohel (1977) based on hominid bone scatters described by Margaret Leakey (1971), and differences in the spatial spread of bones and artefacts such as pottery at American colonial settlements observed by Stanley South (1977, 47–8 and 179–82).

Anyway, a case for greater emphasis on spatial analysis of bone distributions in Britain had been publicly presented for the first time. In the same volume other papers on the sampling of bones and artefacts in spatial dimensions included work in the Upper Thames Valley (Jones 1978 and Wilson 1978a). There was a further report of the English repetition of the African study of bone scavenging (Wilson 1978b, 138).

More fully, further connections between spatial pattern and feature deposit variability were argued from excavations of the Iron Age and Romano–British settlement at Wendens Ambo, Essex. This investigation was undertaken by Paul Halstead, Ian Hodder and Glynis Jones (1978). They concluded generally that the density of bones was greatest near the centre of the settlement – substantiated elsewhere (Wilson 1978a) – and that there were differences in the representation of pottery types and animal species among the bones from the central and peripheral areas of the site. Attention was drawn to differences between bones of species of different size and to differences in the representation of body parts in bone groups.

Importantly, a model of butchery, rubbish disposal, scavenging and bone survival was proposed, probably for the first time in the context of spatial studies in Britain. Unfortunately, the evidence presented in support was inconclusive and the detailed arguments were less convincing. Nevertheless the methodological distinctions made between table, kitchen and butchery material were useful. Nor is it possible to dispute the final remarks of the authors:–

> 'We.... maintain that studies of the type presented here are necessary for the interpretation of archaeological sites and the material from them. ....depending on the type of deposit studied, different results will be obtained in bone and pottery reports.' (Halstead et al 1978, 130)

> 'More extensive modern excavations are not necessarily of greater value unless an attempt is made to understand how different activities are separated [in space] and how refuse was deposited.... It is especially important on small rescue sites to understand the type of rubbish that is being examined before generalisations about the data can be made and comparisons drawn with other sites. As the approach is applied to larger sites there is a clear potential for uncovering larger amounts of information about organisation and functioning within settlements.' (1978, 130–31)

Two studies from Kenya are also of note (Ammerman,

Voorrips & Gifford 1978 and Gifford & Behrensmeyer 1977). Even more relevant was the demonstration by Graeme Barker (1978) of species differences, perhaps related to human group status, in the spreads of bones around Manekweni Zimbabwe in Mozambique.

Limited wider and deeper publication by archaeologists in Britain followed during the next decade. Outside of site reportage, published interests of bone specialists focussed often on how bones came to be deposited (e.g. Fieller, Gilbertson and Ralph 1985) and on socio–economic processes (e.g. Serjeantson and Waldron 1989). Binford (e.g. Binford 1978a and 1981 and Binford & Bertram 1977) and Michael Schiffer (1976, see also 1983) promoted depositional studies overseas, the former notably examining intrasite distribution on Nunamiut Eskimo sites.

Significant differences in the distribution of Romano–British bone deposits at Exeter were noted by Mark Maltby (1979). He (1981) further aided progress by describing Iron Age intrasite variability at Winnall Down, Hampshire, in terms of feature type groups more clearly than previous contrasts noted at Ashville and Appleford sites, Oxfordshire, (Wilson 1978b and 1980a) and Groundwell Farm, Wiltshire (Coy 1981). Cattle and horse bones predominated in the enclosure ditch and the external quarries, whereas sheep and pig bones predominated in the pit group. These differences were ascribed to a combination of differential preservation and disposal practices, particularly of cattle bones stripped of meat.

Simultaneously a useful discussion by Henrietta Moore (1981) was published concerning ethnographic approaches and evidence which suggest how conceptual schemes of cultures have spatial and other consequences for the interpretation of archaeological bones. She gave as instances plots of bone spreads at camps of !Kung bushmen in southern Africa as described by Yellen (1977), and also instanced cultural distributions of bones among the Kalam in New Guinea as described by Ralph Bulmer (1976). Diane Gifford (1980) reviewed other trends observed earlier by Schiffer. Later, in the Sudan Hodder (1982a) studied symbolic and ritual influence in the Nuba practice of rubbish disposal. A chapter by John Wymer (1982) on Palaeolithic house sites and bone debris was transformed by the world–wide work of Binford (1983) on ancient and modern hunter–gatherers and the interpretation of comparable sites and their two-dimensionally recorded finds.

Within *In Pursuit of the Past* (Binford 1983) one should note the informative maps which relate hearths and surroundings of hunting blinds, tents and houses of Nunamiut with spreads of crushed bones and wider accumulations of articulated and less broken bones. Previous analyses of butchery and other related processing of caribou (Binford 1978b and 1981) were put into spatial perspective. Pictorial evidence of this is well illustrated by Fig. 1. Important explanations of the evidence described included the location, cooking and eating of food, the leaving of butchered, cooked and crushed bones, their removal from activity areas by tossing them away, and other wider clearance of bones. Spatial evidence on the

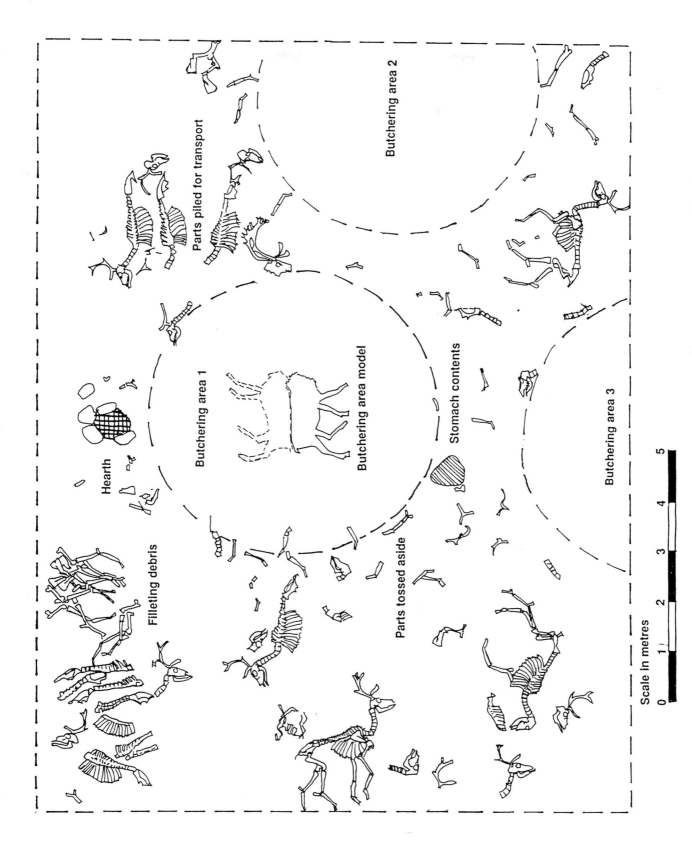

Fig. 1. Structures and bones in the butchering area at the Anavik Springs site, Alaska (after Binford 1983, Fig. 61).

organisation of butchery was also important.

Subsequently, improvements in mapping, computing and statistical methods were made as distributions of bones and artefacts were examined: at Kenyan sites by Ellen Kroll and Isaac (1984) in one paper and by Francoise Hivernal and Hodder (1984) in another; at two American sites, in Oklahoma by Reid Ferring (1984) and in Alaska by Robert Whallon (1984); at Pincevent, France by Ian Johnson (1984); and in the Australian Western Desert by Brian Spurling and Brian Hayden (1984). In the last paper, differences in the spread of small and large bones were briefly discussed. Such differences were made more explicit by an American model of bone spacing proposed by Brian Hesse and Paula Wapnish (1985), Fig. 2, and based on the previously mentioned work by South (1977) and Meadow (1975). The model is an important key, if still questionable quantitatively, to much of the work in this book.

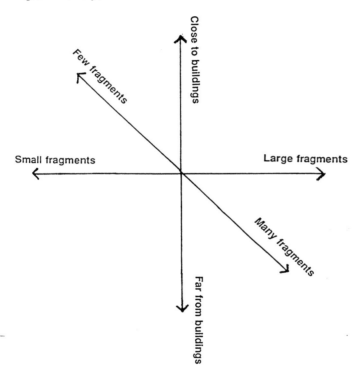

Fig. 2.   Axes of variability on three factors relevant for identifying spaces within an archaeological site that differ in the way bone fragments were accumulated. The factors are: (1) the frequency of bone fragments compared with other categories of debris (diagonal), (2) the relative size of the fragments (horizontal), and (3) the proximity of archaeological features (vertical) (after Hesse and Wapnish 1985, Fig. 86)

With the publication of the Winnall Down report, Maltby (1985a) enlarged on his previous exposition (1981) of site processes by emphasising that the greatest density of bone accumulations was toward the centre of the Iron Age settlement and perhaps of the Roman. Percentages of sheep and pig bones in the Iron Age pits decreased away from the hut locations, possibly a reflection of increasing distance from places of cooking and mutton and pork preparation. Implicit in Maltby's work is the idea that large animals were butchered differently to medium sized ones. For the same settlement, Peter Fasham, mapped distributions of bones and

other debris (1985, Figs. 84–86 and 88). In a review of the same year Maltby (1985b) mentioned spatial differences among faunal remains.

Studies by Jennie Coy (1987) in the Micheldever Wood, Hampshire, report reinforced and developed ideas about site densities of Iron Age bones and differences in species representation between pits and ditches. Indeed much of the relevant British literature has been concerned with explaining feature type variability of bones rather than spatial patterning (later examples include Britnell 1989, 116; Holmes 1993 and Hill 1995, 26), simply because not many authors have perceived bone distributions as manifesting significant spatial patterns. For example, few introductory textbooks on bones discuss this phenomenon to any extent (compare Ryder 1968; Chaplin 1971; Hesse & Wapnish 1985; Davis 1986; Lyman 1994, 415–16 and Rackham 1994, 43). Other studies revealing little spatial patterning include one on Neolithic Woodhenge, Wiltshire (Pollard 1988) and another on the site of Roman Magiovinium (Locker 1987).

Advances, however, were made about this time. One dealt with degraded bones, feature type and spatial patterning of the Iron Age settlement of Mingies Ditch in Oxfordshire (Wilson 1985) and indicated a radial spatial pattern of species bones to be explained. Its genesis will be outlined in chapters 2 to 4 of this book. Elsewhere, information on Romano–British and Saxon spatial patterning and discussion of rubbish disposal was published in the fiche report on Barton Court Farm, Oxfordshire, (Wilson 1986) – see chapter 3. Spatial considerations of house location from the nature of Iron Age bone debris were briefly implicated at Wallingford, Berkshire (Thomas, Robinson, Barratt & Wilson 1986).

Overseas, some of the intrasettlement patterning of Alyawara people in central Australia was analysed by Binford (1987). About the same time Richard Potts (1988, 37–46) reviewed the spatial clustering of bones on African landscapes with respect to distinguishing the Olduvai hominid occupation floors in Tanzania from kill sites of animal predators other than man.

Although the practical emphasis of most British bone specialists has been on investigating feature type variability, vertical stratification of bones has been noted (Gifford & Behrensmeyer 1977; Wilson, Thomas & Wheeler 1979; Hivernal & Hodder 1984); Gifford–Gonzalez et al 1985 and Wilson 1985) and the term 'lateral [i.e. horizontal] variation' has been used, for example by Sebastian Payne (1972) and Maltby (1979) in his study of bones at Exeter and his (1982) examination of the intrasite preservation of sheep and cattle mandibles.

Lateral variation was adopted by Bruce Levitan to describe assemblages from St Katherines Priory, Exeter (1989, 167–73). Since the functions of the rooms were ascertained, the nature of their deposits was of considerable interest. Large bones, chiefly of cattle, were mainly dumped outside the kitchen. Small bones predominated in the dorter, cloisters and elsewhere. Levitan concluded that the large bones were derived from the secondary butchery of carcasses or halved ones in the kitchen. Small bones were categorised as table refuse from eating areas.

Significant steps have been taken in the characterisation of table refuse using modern bone debris and relating similar medieval material to room location and function, particularly domestic activity, in a study of manor house ruins at Hardings Field, Oxfordshire, (Wilson 1989a) – see chapters 7 and 8. Supporting evidence of these patterns was documented for the foundations of the manor house at Faccombe, Wiltshire (Sadler 1990). Sheep, pig and bird bones were relatively abundant in internal occupation layers and less so successively in pits, external layers and ditches, cattle and horse bones being more common in the last named feature types. Peta Sadler suggested that the ditch bones were not primary deposition; kitchen refuse was thrown into yards, and small cooked carcasses were carried whole from the kitchen to the hall for eating.

Another relevant publication is that of an Iron Age enclosure settlement at Watkins Farm, Oxfordshire, (Allen 1990 and Wilson 1990) – chapter 9. The nearby Iron Age settlement of Mingies Ditch, Oxfordshire, has been fully published (Allen & Robinson 1993 and Wilson 1993) and appears another key to understanding spatial relationships of species bones generally, and in relation to the location of houses and hearths – subjects of chapters 4 and 5.

Elsewhere, improved and accurate spatial plots of site debris have been made and discussed for the long barrow of Hazelton North, Gloucestershire (Levitan 1990a) and Bronze Age buildings at Brean Down, Somerset (Levitan 1990b) but few conclusions were reached. Meadow (1991) has reported briefly on bone debris in the town of Harappa, Pakistan. Exhaustively, Hans Peter Blankholm (1991) has re-examined objectively some of the Nunamiut data gathered by Binford at the Mask site, Alaska.

Ethnographic studies of hunter–gatherers and their site refuse have continued to develop under the editorship of Kroll and Douglas Price (1991), especially the spatial analysis of detritus and behaviour of the Kua San in Botswana by Kroll, Lawrence Bartram and Henry Bunn (1991). Examination of bone spreads brought out the importance of the location of site activities generating bone refuse, the intensity of secondary disposal activities, and the intensity of other factors like scavenging and trampling. Modelling which relates such factors emerged in the work of Christopher Carr (1991) and Marc Stevenson (1991). In particular, artefact size sorting processes on sites were comprehensively reviewed by Stevenson and were significant enough to have continued currency as 'McKellar's principle'. His models of activity around hearths depict both the scattering of larger debris outward through dropping, displacement and toss zones, and the trampling and burial of greater amounts of small detritus close to each hearth.

In southern Turkey and Iran a study of nomadic pastoralists and the spatial distribution of artefacts including bones at their temporary settlements has been undertaken by Roger Cribb (1991, 126–32 and 172–82). Areas with greater amounts of head debris were thought to indicate butchery locations and appeared discernable from [domestic] discard groups which were characterised by bone scrap.

Further, the concept of taphonomic space developed by Hesse and Wapnish (1985, 90–92, based on work by Francois Poplin (1975) and others, has recently been extended by Jack Hofman and James Enloe (1992) in editing a collection of papers on refitting studies of bones and stones, mainly at American sites. Of particular relevance is the analysis of data at the Bugas–Holding site in Wyoming where David Rapson and Lawrence Todd (1992, 240) demonstrated that the spreads of conjoining bones around hearths differed between bighorn sheep and bison, bones of the latter being spread over a wider area than the former. Provided explanations were tentative.

In summary, the well read bone specialist may already have discerned general spatial patterns of interest from the highlighted evidence and papers listed here. The general reader, however, may be forgiven for concluding that the literature of bone work demonstrates an uneven patchwork of spatial evidence and relevant ideas and shows few comprehensive interpretive and explanatory models (although the pertinence, development and influence of the listed contributions of workers in the field should become apparent as the pages of this book are turned). Moreover, frustration was expressed in 1990 about the slow publication and poor availability of the larger reports and papers relating to spatial investigations of site debris (Wilson 1994). Some years after such comments, a substantial corpus of work is gradually being published and responded to (e.g. Wilson 1993; Wilson & Edwards 1993; Woodward & Leach 1993 and Hill 1995, 24–30).

To further rectify this some stagnation of awareness, a book on the subject appears not only useful but can reveal a significant realm of investigation which adds to, and complements, the emerging dimensional framework of bone analysis. Valuable insight into human activity can be made by amalgamating results of studies at sites in central southern Britain. Hopefully, these insights will become clear during the development of a set of descriptive and explanatory ideas in a site to site programme of examining archaeological phenomena.

Chapter 2

Regional Archaeology in The Upper Thames Valley and an Introduction to the Bone Work there

Having reviewed the world–wide literature on the spatial patterning of animal bones, we will now turn to the background archaeology of the region I worked in to study the bone collections. Investigation of archaeological sites has been carried out within the south Midlands county of Oxfordshire and the edge of Gloucestershire, commonly called the Upper Thames Valley. Most of the excavations involved took place in the vicinity of Oxford and all major digs were located within 40 km of it, Fig. 3.

Typically most of the sites occurred on the gravel terraces or adjacent ground of the Thames or other river systems. Background geology, environments, cultures and history of this region have been described in a number of previous publications (Martin & Steele 1954, Briggs, Cook & Rowley 1986 and Robinson & Wilson 1987.

Digging and publication of excavations in the Upper Thames region has had a long but chequered history. Productivity in terms of excavation, especially, and of publication reflects national trends and has increased enormously during the last two or three decades. This growth is primarily a response to the continued destruction of archaeological sites as a result of town and road developments and the quarrying of gravel and other rock.

Such rescue excavations and some research archaeology have been funded by the Department of Environment, English Heritage, Manpower Services Commission, commercial firms like Amey Roadstone Corporation, and City, Town, District and County Councils. Various archaeological groups have been involved in the excavation of sites but the most important in the region has been the Oxford Archaeological Unit, which was formed in 1974.

Rescue archaeology created an awareness of its deficiences of method and an imperative for adequate scientific and other research. The ultimate aim of local rescue and research methods was the proper understanding of the very diverse cultural heritage which developed beside a historic river and its wider region.

In order to derive the maximum academic and public benefits from excavations, strategies and objectives of Oxford Unit excavations evolved the following policies:–

1. Longterm planning and anticipation of threatened sites.
2. Emphasis on preparing archaeological ground surveys, such as of cropmarks and urban sites.
3. Incorporation of environmental archaeology studies within more conventional archaeology.
4. Utilisation of sampling techniques in conjunction with large scale excavations.
5. Recognition of a total landscape archaeology in which excavations were situated.

Naturally these policies were not unrelated to the development of spatial studies of bones. They provide a context in which science trained and excavation–conscious graduates were brought together as environmental archaeologists and helped to produce some early publication successes (Parrington 1978 and Lambrick & Robinson 1979) and subsequently influenced teamwork and research objectives of future digs.

Early reports written about animal bones were few, usually sparse in data, and primitive in understanding. From later descriptive reports, which presented useful species and skeletal data and modest analysis of the evidence, grew the full scale priorities of bone work.

In order to assess ancient animal husbandry and human cultural economies, values and rituals, the research requirements were extremely diverse and demanding. The underlying knowledge required ranged from studies of animal disease and carcass butchery to the identification of the age and sex of slaughtered beasts as is detailed in Table 1. To meet these interests, knowledge from a variety of geological, biological, anthropological, historical and other subject disciplines was required and sooner or later was applied to the scrutiny of bones and data collection. These fields which impinged on bone work have been somewhat casually but conveniently lumped together with it as environmental archaeology. A review of regional findings in this new science up until 1983 is available (Robinson & Wilson 1987).

At the beginning of writing reports on bones, it was not always clear which was the most important and reliable information to collect, for example in determinations of age and sex. Some confusion came too as opinions on methods of data collection and analysis fluctuated, especially in the all important debate over how animal abundance at settlements should be estimated from the remaining bones.

In summary, most bone workers knew what findings it would be useful to announce and discuss in our reports but the issues were complicated, especially as we became aware of a new topic in the making: taphonomy, the many cultural and biological pathways by which animal skeletons of meat carcasses were disarticulated, broken, moved and buried in archaeological deposits.

The difficulties of understanding the taphonomy of bones were problems springing from the largely inductive (or data collecting) science we practiced first. Later, at the opposing theoretical and hypothetico–deductive pole of investigations, some of us also became aware of deficiencies in the overview by which bone specialists and other environmental archaeologists approached our discipline:–

Where bones are discussed it would be inept to treat them in the context of 'the physical

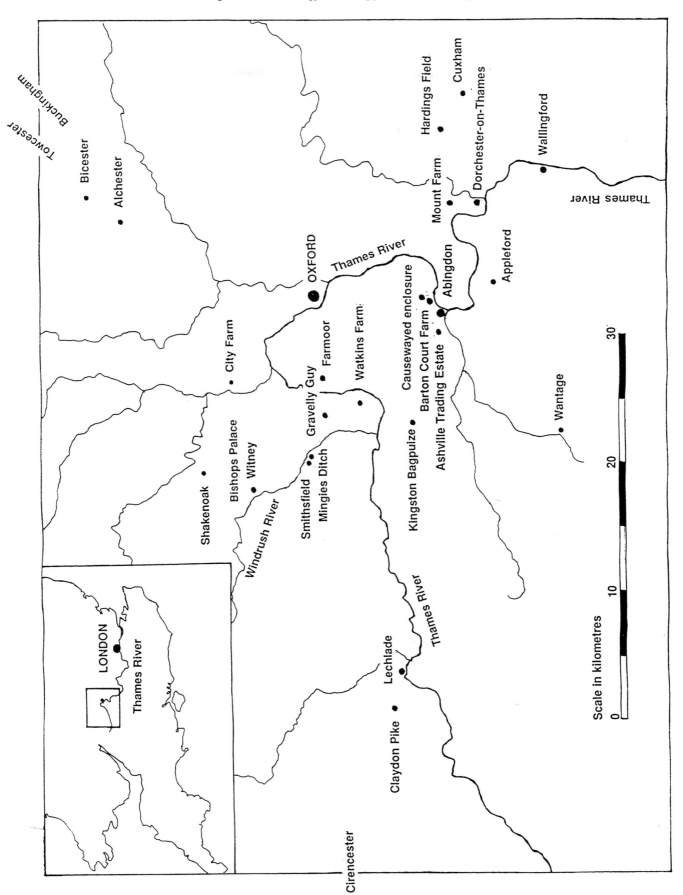

Fig. 3. Location map of archaeological sites in the Upper Thames Valley.

surroundings of man' as constitutes the self imposed limits of a number of authors and their useful purpose in defining environmental archaeology. Not only do studies of human bones thus rest in a conceptual limbo but the majority of animal bones simply appear to represent the physical surroundings of a species whose characteristics do not change. Yet not only is it known that there evolved profound [ly intricate] relationships of man with domesticated plants and animals but these very relationships help to define the ecological status of each ethnic group of man. The relationships should explain the separation of cultural and natural communities and the ability of people to modify their physical surroundings.' (Robinson & Wilson 1987, 25)

Thus, *'Our emphasis is upon past human activity which often related a number of distinctive ecosystems and thus evolved a higher level of biological and social organisation. The overall and special considerations can be termed ecocultural. An ecoculture is here defined as the fundamental organisation of each type of society and the particular ecosystems to which it is dynamically or passively associated. We see the purpose of environmental archaeology as helping to characterise each distinctive ecoculture and ...... tracing the environmental developments which took place in the region.'* (1987, 22)

Although the idea of ecoculture is still nebulous in its practical application, it seems to legitimise the crossing of interdisciplinary boundaries to allow new intellectual entities to be created and which were intuitively sensed to arise from a closer examination of bone data and its spatial patterning. Certainly, by definition, each ecoculture can be imagined to imprint or cast its particular spatial patterns on the bones during their rending and eventual deposition.

It remains for these spatial patterns to be demonstrated in this book. After that it might be possible to deduce how one ecoculture is similar to others or different from them.

Table 1 The potential and limitations of bone analysis and how observations might be related to more complex ideas at several levels of investigation

RAW DATA	INFORMATION by relatively direct inference or statistical evaluation	INTERPRETATIVE DISCUSSION OR THEORETICAL RECONSTRUCTRUCTION by inference and circumstantantial evidence
Lab. examination	Contexts of excavation, field studies, etc.	Experimental reconstruction, historical data, etc.
IDENTIFICATION OF SPECIES AND SKELETAL ELEMENTS, BONE NUMBERS, WEIGHTS, MEASUREMENTS, TOOTH ERUPTION AND WEAR, EPIPHYSIAL FUSION, SEXUAL DIMORPHISM, ETC. Collection bias or sample control	(A) Pathways to deposition of bones 1 SPECIES SELECTION FOR EATING 2 BUTCHERY OF CARCASSES 3 BONE USAGE OR WASTAGE 4 EFFECTS OF SCAVENGING AND TRAMPLING 5 DIFFERENTAL BONE DECAY 6 EFFECTS OF INTRUSIVE SPECIES (B) The original animal populations Estimates biased by (A) 1 RELATIVE ABUNDANCE OF ANIMAL SPECIES Accuracy? 2 SIZE AND VARIABILITY OF SPECIES Approximate 3 PROPORTION OF SEXES Difficult to separate 4 DEVELOPMENTAL STAGES Approximate age at slaughtering or death from other causes 5 PATHOLOGY Difficult to diagnose 6 AGE AND SEX STRUCTURE OF LIVE POPULATIONS	(C) Our concepts of cultural phenomena 1 EXTENT AND NATURE OF ENVIRONMENT A1, B1 2 IMPORTANCE OF EACH SPECIES FOR CALORIE AND PROTEIN YIELD B1, B2, C6 3 ABUNDANCE OF MEAT(?) AND VARIETY OF DIET A2, A3, B1, B4 4 LOCATION OF BUTCHERY AND EATING OF FOOD 5 RUBBISH DISPOSAL A2, A3, A4. 6 FUNCTION OF INDIVIDUAL ANIMAL IN HERD/FLOCK - meat, wool, dairy A1, B1, B2, B3 7 PASTORAL RELATIONSHIPS, e.g. winter feeding; effect of arable farming 8 SEASONAL SLAUGHTER/OCCUPATION 9 IMPORT- EXPORT OF MEAT, e.g. marketing 10 BREEDING CHANGES AND/OR IMPORTATION OF STOCK B2 11 RITUAL PRACTICES

From Wilson, Grigson and Payne 1982 (1974).

PART II

STUDIES TO DEVELOP MODELS OF HUMAN AND NATURAL ACTIVITY AT SIMPLER RURAL SETTLEMENTS

...... at least some human activities will be spatially separated within most places of occupation....... (Whallon 1973, 116, emphasis given by Binford 1983, 238).

......a pattern does underlie the spatial distribution of specific activities; the location or locations in which an activity takes place are not scattered at random, and the byproducts from many kinds of activities do form clusters that one can distinguish......(Yellen 1977, 95).

Spatial analysis is a logical extension of ordinary aspatial analysis in any applied science which has a spatial component of variability (Hietala 1984b, 3).

Chapter 3

Discovering Spatial Patterns

The background literature of bones has been centred on a geographical region of investigation and to some aims and policies of rescue and research archaeology, including environmental archaeology and the work on animal bones. Now this chapter brings together the programme of regional site excavations with some early results of the bone work both ancient and modern.

While our publication aims were fairly clear, putting scientific methods into practice and working systematically through a set of excavation and post–excavation problems was rarely straight forward. Work on bones was often dictated by rescue demands of digging sites of different type and period, and influenced by the progress of stratigraphical, phasing and dating studies necessary to categorise site features and bone groups for analysis. So continuity of regional research interests amounted to approximate long term planning and unstated expectations which were frequently delayed by the short–term schedule of reporting of bone collections from an uneven succession of sites and digging seasons.

Although the somewhat chaotic flavour of reporting on bones will no doubt emerge in this book, a purely piecemeal account of regional bonework would be tedious and confusing. Equally a purely thematic account would not capture the development of methods from site to site.
By way of compromise between these alternative narrative plots, the text will first focus on the spatial exploration of the smaller, simpler and rural settlement sites, leaving the larger and more complicated rural settlement sites and urban ones until later. This plot has the merit of reflecting another early Oxford Unit excavation policy: not simply moving on to dig the next site to be threatened with destruction but rather to select as diverse a range of prehistoric and Roman sites as possible within the available budget.

In practice, most excavations in the region had been small to medium sized affairs, at least to begin with. If a second or third season of digging was feasible, well and good. But the Unit became able to plan better in the longer term, and more ambitious and extensive excavations were undertaken.

Digging on the most informative sites began in Abingdon in 1972, where the first season of excavation commenced at the multiperiod but chiefly Roman site of Barton Court Farm on behalf of the Abingdon Excavation Committee. Two years later, excavations began at the Iron Age and Roman Ashville Trading–Estate site, Abingdon, and digging, post–excavation work and publication by the Oxford Unit were achieved in four years (Parrington 1978). Barton Court Farm reporting took longer to integrate findings and publish (Miles 1986). Iron Age Mingies Ditch, Hardwick with Yelford, was mainly dug in 1977–78 (Allen & Robinson 1993). Neolithic to Saxon Mount Farm site, Berinsfield, occupied a similar period of excavation (Lambrick unpub.). Medieval manor remains at Hardings Field, Chalgrove, were excavated over

a slightly later period (Page et. al. unpub.), while digging at Iron Age and Roman Lechlade and Claydon Pike began in 1979 and ended around 1983 (Miles & Palmer in prep.).

Relevant excavations in the old towns of Oxford and Abingdon followed a parallel though sporadic schedule from 1967 onwards, Church Street excavations (Hassall, Halpin & Mellor 1984 and 1989) being the major intensively dug site. Other sites which contribute to spatial studies will be mentioned as necessary in later stages of this book.

–0–

Although previous site reports boosted the understanding of regional ecocultural phenomena, for example the Shakenoak Roman villa publications (Brodribb, Hands & Walker 1968–78), the examination of the bones at the Ashville Trading Estate, Abingdon, was the first work to attract my attention to a new set of interpretative problems.

Mike Parrington (1978) and others have described the intensively occupied site of this Iron Age hamlet or village of round houses, outbuildings, drainage gullies and storage pits, Fig. 4. Grain growing and cattle and sheep keeping were major farming activities of the Celtic people there.

Of additional curiosity were apparently unexplainable anomalies in the presentation of my results. In routine reporting of archaeological bones, differences between data grouped according to culture and chronological period are, not unreasonably, assumed to be interpretable according to those categories of meaning. That is, any differences in results would be thought due to a change of culture and,or economy.

It appears more complicated and less conceivable, however, that the site results would vary according to the qualities and quantities of bones and pottery dug out from features of different type. With the Ashville results, I decided to summarise evidence by adding bone data from pits and ditches separately, simply because these were the main types of feature at the site. The percentage representation of bones of different species differed between the feature groups. Sheep bones were relatively more common in pit groups than in ditch groups, especially during the middle period of occupation. By contrast, cattle and horse bones were relatively abundant in the ditch and gully groups, Table 2. Differences in the species representation of skeletal elements were also noted between these feature type groups.

These were the kind of anomalies which might be passed over by investigators, especially those with a backlog of many boxes of bones to deal with, but somehow they stimulated questions. Various explanations were offered, including the distributional differences being due to patterns of a) variable bone retrieval from the soil, b) bone preservation, and c) fragmentation and scattering of bones by

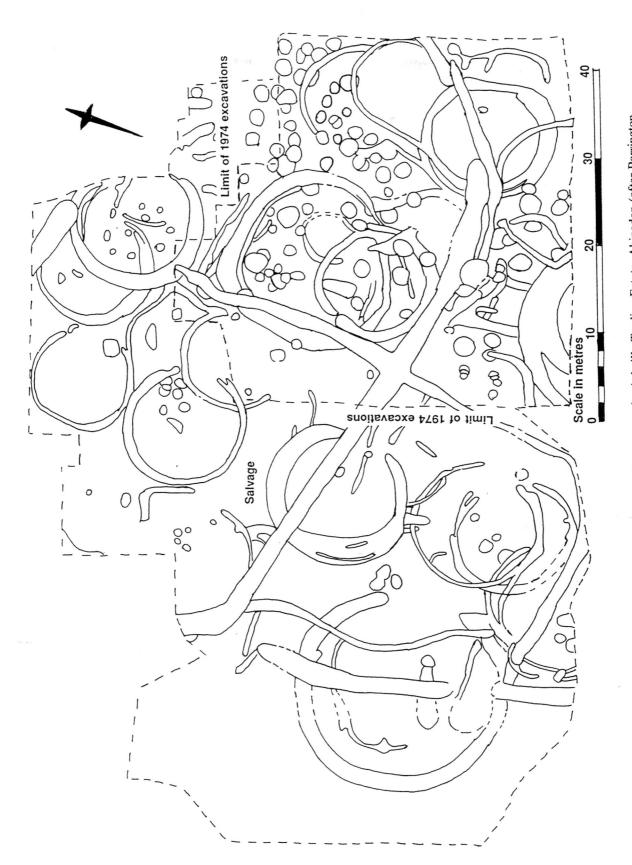

Fig. 4. Plan of the Iron Age features and excavation area at the Ashville Trading Estate, Abingdon (after Parrington 1978).

butchery and scavenging. Too many explanations were possible for the same basic evidence.

With hindsight, one reason for this inconclusiveness was that no adequate idea of the spatial spread of the bones was obtained. For example, the complex of intercutting and overlaid features was not dug widely enough to define the boundaries of the Iron Age settlement, Fig. 4. And, although there was evidence of regularly spaced houses and coherent groups of features, most recovery of bones was confined to the smaller and more complicated area of the 1974 excavations. Lastly, during the 1970s it was not obvious to bone experts that the spatial patterning of bones was an important part of the effective analysis of bone collections.

–0–

Differences found at Ashville between feature type deposits might have been dismissed later as an inconsequential oddity. However, the pattern recurred during the examination of other bone collections, for example at the late Bronze Age and Iron Age occupation site at Appleford, investigated in 1973 (Hinchliffe & Thomas 1980 and Wilson 1980a, Table II). The supporting evidence reinforced the need to obtain more meaningful information to explain how and why the difference occurred.

–0–

Having caught up a little on background reading in 1974, my imagination was stirred by the work of Glynn Isaac (1967 and 1971) in Kenya where he investigated the effects of scavenging and other natural processes on bones exposed to the weather and wild animals. From a central dump of bone refuse, it was found that scavengers like hyaenas completely destroyed many bones and scattered larger bones farther than smaller ones.

My fieldwork repeated the work of Isaac under English skies, on waste ground at Daisybank and Barton Court Farm, Abingdon, where dogs were walked, foxes prowled and crows foraged.

Small groups of cooked and uncooked bones and fragments were left next to marker stakes on exposed gravel surfaces, on short grass turf, on leafmouldy ground below trees, in emptied shallow post–holes and in one deep pit. Bones exposed on the ground surfaces were usually scattered or carried off by scavengers within a few days. Those bones in one post–hole 20 cm deep were partly dug out and partly buried by a dog or fox. Those in the deep pit remained untouched.

Most bones left on the surface simply disappeared from experimental view or were difficult to locate when carried more than 10 m from their sources. One fragment was found 20 m from the original dumping place.

Small and non meaty or little marrowed bones tended to be left near their sources. Larger bones either were carried off completely or were scattered some metres or more, in

several cases being pecked about by birds.

Thus it seems inevitable that fresh bones will be moved outwards from where they are dumped by people. Bones tend to be sorted by size and tend to end up in different spatial zones, large ones tending to occupy the dump site periphery and small ones in more central areas.

A brief account of this work was entered at the end of the Ashville bone report (Wilson 1978b 138). The findings hovered in my mind whenever thinking about bone distributions but no other site bone distribution fitted the pattern until results were collated for Barton Court Farm between 1975 and 1978.

–0–

The successive rural settlements of Barton Court Farm sprawled over a wide area. Extensive excavation was facilitated by the shallowness of much of the topsoil lying over the gravel of the river terrace.

Soil stripping and digging soon revealed a late Iron Age enclosure ditch and house site which were succeeded first by the features of several phases of a large Romano–British farmhouse and farmyard, and second by the remnants of a Saxon hamlet. Evidence of pastoral farming (e.g. of dung beetles) was very abundant while interesting evidence of arable farming (e.g. carbonised cereals), woodland and riverine environments also occurred (Miles 1986).

Cattle bones were more abundantly found in the Iron Age and Roman deposits than at Ashville. Nevertheless similar differences in the representation of common species from the ditches and pits or pitlike features were found for Iron Age, Romano–British and Saxon groups of bones, as shown in Table 3 (Wilson 1986, Table 5). The contrast between the results is greater if the frequencies of cattle and horse bones are added together and compared with summed frequencies of sheep and pig. This indicated that the size of bones and fragments was a major factor in determining the composition of species bones in features of different type.

Percentage representation of the two largest species among the four commonest species, grouped by area, feature type and period were plotted on a simplified site plan as shown in Fig. 5. This demonstrated a greater feature type variation in species representation than that indicated by the pit versus ditch comparison in Table 3.

Examination of the results for the Romano–British ditches showed particularly that the percentage of sheep and pig bones in the rectangular enclosure ditch around the Romano–British house was greater than in the ditches of the surrounding farmyard. In addition, when measurements of anciently broken fragments from these deposits were compared, the average size of cattle and horse bones differed between the rectangular ditch (means of 8.2 and 8.7 cm) and the surrounding farmyard ditches (11.1 and 14.4 cm). Thus the proportion of cattle and horse bones and of large bone fragments in the sample groups generally increased as the

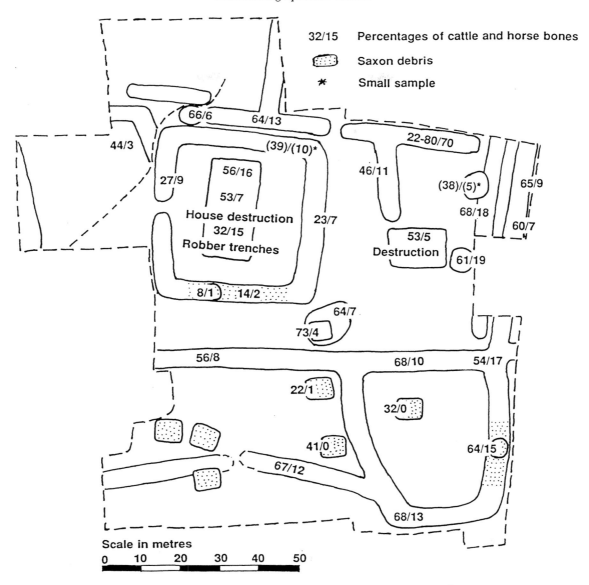

Fig. 5.   Stylised plan of major features and percentages of cattle and horse among the groups of Romano–British and Saxon bones at Barton Court Farm (from Wilson 1986).

distance of the farmyard ditches from the house increased.

This generalisation was qualified by a higher representation of cattle and horse among the demolition debris from the robber trenches and the infilled cellar of the house. Such later debris might not reflect the distribution of bones in and immediately adjacent to the household when it was active. The zone within the rectangular house ditch may have been kept clear of large bones during the main occupation phase of the house.

Scavenging activities like those noted above in the field study might have created such a distribution. Rubbish clearance of large bones and the butchery of large carcasses away from the house were also thought to explain much of the spatial distribution of bones. Many large bones had been dumped into a well some distance from the house although the debris could have come from a small Late Roman building near the well. Articulated bones of cattle and horse survived in some farmyard ditches and in a pit lying just

outside the rectangular ditch which suggested direct dumping of rubbish. Direct disposal of bones to dogs was also indicated by evidence of their skeletons being buried whole close to the farmhouse and the yards.

Saxon bone debris had a similar configuration to the Romano–British material although cattle and horse were less well represented among the Saxon bone collection. Pig and sheep bones were mainly found in the pits of the Saxon sunken huts, and also inserted into one section of the rectangular Roman ditch. Other concentrations, predominantly of cattle and horse, were found farther away in a wickerwork well and in an adjacent ditch.

This Saxon distribution was not entirely clear in its meaning. Strictly it could not be concluded that the bones originated from household activity in all or most of the sunken huts as several of them contained very few bones – anyway most domestic activity was thought to have taken place in longhouses which had uncertain status and location on the site. Additionally, the large accumulation of bones in one hut pit included offcuts of antler which indicated waste from bone working. Most probably these bones were dumped in or near the sunken hut after it went out of use.

A revealing glimpse of scavenging or rubbish clearance was obtained while calculating Minimum Numbers of Individual animal species among the Saxon bones. Two halves of a red deer radius were found to fit each other perfectly. They had been uncovered 35 m apart, one half in the Saxon well and the other in a sunken hut. They indicated sizeable outward movements from the bone dump but alternative pathways are possible too. Nevertheless one was reminded of the scavenging studies again.

By and large only an uncertain outline could be given of the human and other animal activities which brought about the observed differences in the bone deposition. The most important finding, however, was the recognition of the potential value of spatial evidence in the explanation of the variation of feature type deposits.

Table 2 **Percentages of bone fragment frequency in Iron Age features at Ashville Trading Estate, Abingdon, Oxfordshire**

	Pits					Ditches				
Phase	1	2	3	Other	Total	1	2	3	Other	Total
Fragment number	464	312	93	414	1283	13	947	657	468	2085
	%	%	%	%	%	%	%	%	%	%
Sheep/goat	52	70	48	62	59	–	54	44	56	51
Cattle	33	19	38	23	27	–	32	39	32	34
Pig	10	8	10	12	10	–	9	12	7	9
Horse	4	3	3	3	3	–	4	5	4	5
Dog	2	–	1	–	1	–	1	–	1	1

From Wilson 1978b.

Table 3 **Percentages of bone fragment frequency in ditches and pitlike features at Barton Court Farm, Abingdon, Oxfordshire**

	'Pits'				Ditches				
Period/ cent. AD.	Iron Age	Roman 1-2	3-4	Saxon	Iron Age	Roman 1-2	3-4	4-5	Saxon
Fragment number	70	10	315	308	813	324	1624	785	68
	%	%	%	%	%	%	%	%	%
Sheep/goat	46	–	42	33	39	26	29	19	13
Cattle	33	–	52	35	46	49	50	64	62
Pig	12	–	11	32	8	12	8	8	6
Horse	9[1]	–	6	1	7	13	13	9	19

[1] = Excluding 21 bones from distal ends of 2 horse legs
From Wilson 1986.

Chapter 4

Configuration of Occupation Debris at the Iron Age House Enclosure Site of Mingies Ditch

As the bone report on findings at Barton Court Farm approached its first draft in 1977, a new opportunity arose to explore spatial patterning. Gravel quarrying was scheduled to destroy an enigmatic cropmark site close to Hardwick with Yelford, near Stanton Harcourt, Oxfordshire, and alongside the River Windrush, a tributary of the Thames. The locality was called Mingies Ditch. From aerial photographs the cropmark consisted of two concentric enclosure ditches and ditches of a trackway which entered the enclosure.

Although the period and type of occupation were uncertain, the site offered five advantages for the investigation of spatial patterning of any occupation debris.

a)   The size of the settlement was about 90 m in diameter and a fairly complete excavation of it was feasible.

b)   Unlike previously excavated sites at Ashville and Barton Court Farm, it appeared that the occupation area was defined and limited by the enclosure ditches. It was probable that any house sites within were few in number and uncomplicated in their spatial arrangement.

c)   The coherence and size of the cropmark indicated a single and perhaps short occupation and this would simplify the interpretation of site debris.

d)   The excavators proposed to record the position of all artefacts and bones to within squares or 'quadrats' measuring 2 m x 2 m, an improvement on previous excavation methods in the region.

e)   As the site lay in meadowland, the upper soil layers were believed to be little disturbed by ploughing so that shallow features and occupation layers, but not necessarily bones, were preserved better than at ploughsoil sites.

Mingies Ditch appeared to provide the first opportunity for a bone specialist in the region to help plan the overall strategy of the excavation and assist in implementing it. Normally, the bone-person had been involved at the post-excavation stage and in giving minor advice on soil sieving during digging.

Unfortunately, excavation funding was limited and the effort of the first digging season was directed towards conventional priorities of obtaining stratigraphy and dating evidence and, less conventionally, to the retrieval of waterlogged remains. Sampling of the density of bones in the occupation deposits was possible, providing I sieved the soil myself.

As excavations with Oxford University Archaeological Society students advanced, the site director Mark Robinson and his assistant Tim Allen established that there were house foundations within the enclosure ditches and that the settlement had flourished during the Iron Age (Robinson & Allen 1978, Allen 1981 and Allen & Robinson 1979).

While ultimately large areas of the settlement were excavated (Allen & Robinson 1993), the early commencement of sieving made it impossible to select my sample locations at random in sectioned features. Yet it was felt soil samples would be fairly typical of each area of the site sampled. Bucketfuls of deposits were dug out of sectioned features and sieved for bones by washing the sticky silts and gravel through a large homemade 6 mm sieve – the aim was to set a standard for the recovery of mammal bones rather than to retrieve the smallest bones like those of fish.

Results of sieving were unspectacular but were quickly published in a survey of innovative sampling methods in Britain (Wilson 1978a). The results, Fig. 6, provided timely quantification of the assertion of Halstead and his coworkers that the density of occupation debris falls off toward the periphery of a settlement (chapter 1). An exception was a small secondary concentration of bones at the entrance to the enclosure. Analysis of the normally excavated bones and pottery was to confirm these findings.

Excavation extended to a second season with scanty finances and supported by student labour. Building foundations, hearths and four-post structures within the enclosure indicated a succession of up to seven houses, perhaps only one family living there at any one time. Organic remains indicated a pastoral environment with some scrub or hedges encircling the settlement, see Fig. 7.

To me, the arrangement of features suggested some general radial symmetry in the layout and functioning of the settlement. A roughly circular gravel embankment lay inside most of the inner enclosure ditch. House sites formed an irregular ring inside the bank and around a central area into which opened the ditches of the radially aligned inner trackway.

Relevant aims of bone analysis were:–

1.   To describe the principal variation in the spatial distribution of bones.

2.   To make general predictions about the different bone distributions to be expected and, from the results, to advance ideas on the processes of bone dispersal which might be tested by studies elsewhere.

About a year after the second season of digging finished, I recorded the bones according to the feature and quadrat in which they were found. Most bones were in a poor state of preservation since many had come from relatively superficial occupation layers which normally would have been destroyed by ploughing. Their recovery was therefore a bonus to studying site bone distributions but, since most of the less robust skeletal elements had been destroyed, it seemed that some aspects of bone related activity could not be investigated properly. However, it was a matter of

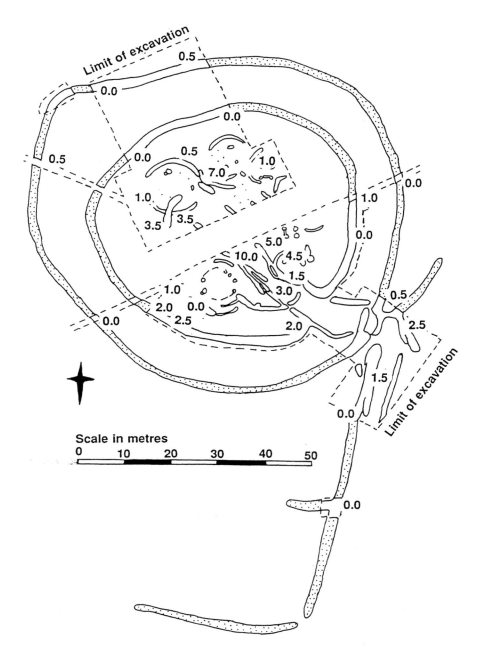

Fig. 6. Site distribution of the average number of bones per bucketful of soil at Mingies Ditch (from Wilson 1978a).

pressing on and seeing what could be managed. Some of the preconceptions about bone dispersal were:–

a)   Site bones came from animals slaughtered on the site. Thus discussion ought to discern where they were killed.

b)   Carcass dismemberment followed the butchery described at Iron Age Ashville.

c)   Butchery stages were less differentiated in time and place than in urban contexts where a division of labour during butchery and consumption leaves distinctive wastes.

d)   Defleshing of large carcasses would leave most of the bones in a semi–articulated state some distance from the hearths.

e)   Burnt bones were expected in the vicinity of hearths and houses.

f)   Many bones, particularly large ones, would have been moved considerable distances by scavengers. Such bones might not be distinguishable from bones cleared by people from areas of activity but both processes might be indicated by comparison with pottery distributions which would not be spread as far as the bones.

g)   Worked bones would be artefacts less subject to scavenging and rubbish clearance (being smaller, less odious etc.) and would not be spread far from their cultural sources.

The simplest general approach to spatial analysis appeared to be the examination of the observed radial symmetry and its concentric distribution of bones and other debris at the

Fig. 7.   Artist's impression of the settlement at Mingies Ditch (after P. Hughes in Allen and Robinson 1993).

settlement. With these preconceptions in mind, expected trends of bone and artefactual debris toward the centre or the periphery of the site were postulated as given in Table 4.

calculated and drawn out on transparent paper at the same scale as in the site plan.

Table 4 Hypothetical trends of radial distributions of bones outwards from the centre of the settlement of Mingies Ditch

Material	Central (c) or peripheral (p) trend predicted	Affected by scavenging	Affected by rubbish clearance	Cultural activity implied
Potsherds	c	no	little	diverse
Total bone frequency	c	yes	–	?main focus
Burnt bone	c	no	little	fireplaces ?cooking
Large bones	p	most of all	most of all	?butchery
Teeth and metapodials'	c e.g. sheep p e.g. cattle	yes (teeth) yes(indirectly)	large bones & large species	?early stages of butchery
Humerus and femur'.²	c	yes	large bones & large species	?late stages of butchery
Worked bones	c	no	little	usage or manufacturing
Anomalous deposits	c e.g. horse skulls p e.g. entranceway	not if buried	not detectable	ritual

' = Skeletal element trends largely unable to be investigated
² = Later enlarged to include scapula, pelvis and consideration of vertebrae
From Wilson 1993.

–0–

Some months elapsed and the location of my work was moved in 1980 from the annexe of the Archaeological Unit to the old zoology lab in the University Museum, Oxford. Getting back to business there, I began analysis of the data from Mingies Ditch, at first in conventional ways of report preparation.

It was not possible to make a pit versus ditch contrast as storage pits were absent from the lowlying site. However, bones of sheep and pig were found to be very abundant in the superficial occupation layers and internal trackway ditches while cattle and horse bones were more abundant in other ditches, gullies and 'bathshaped pits'. Since the occupation layers occurred centrally, this was the first indication of the spatial pattern of bones.

Then, secondly and unconventionally, in order to substantiate the spatial pattern, I transferred the bone data to a plan of the grid squares from which the bones had originated. It was then a matter of constructing a concentric sampling pattern that fitted over the site plan at the same scale as the grid pattern of 2 m x 2 m quadrats. Due consideration was given to factors of site area, sample size and properties of the layout of the sampling pattern or template. The best compromise appeared to be a sample size area of 320 square metres or 80 of the 2 m x 2 m quadrats of the site grid system. The concentric form of the sample areas was

To begin with, square graph paper was used. On this the first 80 squares or quadrats were allocated by addition to a nucleus of a central square. Outermost quadrats were added to infill places at the smallest radial distance from the central quadrat so that the boundary of the sample area formed an approximately circular form. Quadrats of the succeeding sample areas were added on in a similar manner until the excavated area on the plan was covered by the sampling scheme. Then each concentric sample area was outlined on tracing paper above the squared pattern by tracing and inking along the outer boundary of each successive group of 80 quadrats.

This latter transparent sampling template was overlaid and aligned on the grid system of the site plan, centred approximately on the area within the irregular ring of houses, and finally aligned on the major features so that each type, especially the enclosure ditches, lay as much as possible within one or two of the sample area rings. Fig 8 shows the final alignment of the sampling template on the site plan. Privately I called the sampling template 'the Mingies mandala' because of its similarity to Eastern religious schemata for contemplative purposes. There was plenty to think about this one!

Data of bone debris recorded within each sample area were then counted into result groups which occurred at increasing radial distances from the centre of the site. Most pertinently

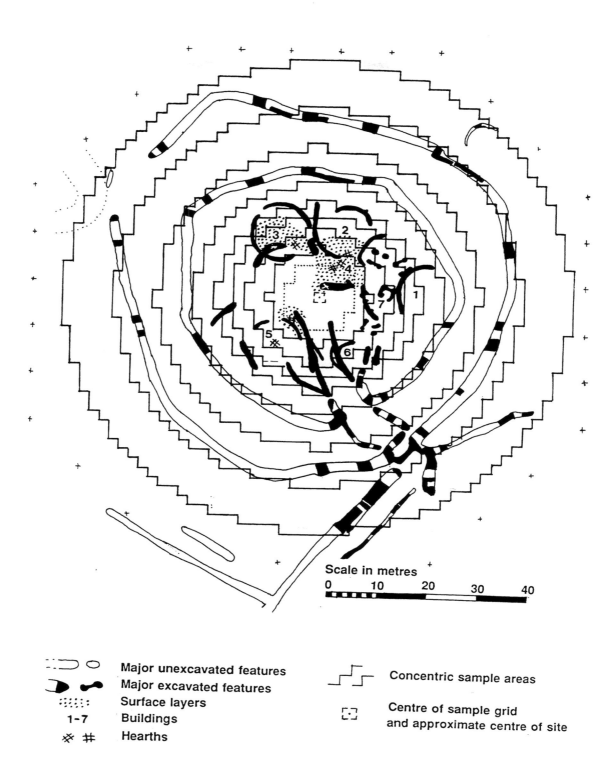

Scale in metres

0   10   20   30   40

Symbol	Description
Major unexcavated features	
Major excavated features	
Surface layers	
1-7	Buildings
Hearths	
Concentric sample areas	
Centre of sample grid and approximate centre of site	

Fig. 8. Concentric sample area template superimposed on the plan of features at Mingies Ditch (after Wilson 1993).

Table 5 Percentages of species bones outward from the centre
of the site (concentric sample pattern)

Sample numbers	Mean distance from centre of of site (m)	Fragment number	Sheep/ goat %	Pig %	Cattle %	Horse %
1	7.2	698	67	4	23	6
2	12.4	363	59	10	22	9
3	16.0	278	50	9	33	8
4	18.9	158	15	9	48	28
5-6[1]	22.6	52	25	2	31	42
7-10[2]	28.6	75	25	5	47	23
11-16[3]	36.4	58	29	2	55	14
17-25[4]	45.7	19	47	5	26	21
		Total 1701				

Peripheral sample areas have been added together to increase the
sample size of their results. These aggregated samples cover
approximately the area of the following features:
[1] = Peripheral occupation area and bank
[2] = Inner enclosure ditch
[3] = Most of outer enclosure ditch
[4] = Antennae ditches and part of outer enclosure
From Wilson 1993.

Table 6 **Some comparable cumulative percentages of site debris in
concentric sample groups**

Sample group numbers	n	c/p	1	1-3	1-5	1-7
Bone offcuts	5	c	80	100	-	-
Worked bone & antler	10	c	70	90	100	-
Pot fabrics A & B	>1000	c	45-47	92-95	97-98	97-98
Burnt artefactual debris	54-161	c	33-42	70-94	74-96	90-100
Burnt bones	61-322	c	54-59	90-98	97-98	97-98
Sheep	903	c	52	91	94	96
Cattle	504	p	33	60	85	89
Horse	191	p	21	50	84	90
Bones 10-20 cm	182	p	28	55	76	85
Bones >20 cm	41	p	20	49	68	78

n = Number of items
c/p = Predicted central/peripheral trend (Table 4)
From Wilson 1993.

the species composition by number and density of bones within these sample areas was found to vary enormously as Table 5 shows.

Sheep and pig bones predominated at the centre of the site where bones were particularly numerous. Toward the site periphery bone spreads thinned out and bones of cattle and horse were prominent. Other trends of site debris are presented in Table 6 as accumulating percentages of each type of debris moving from central to peripheral sample zones of the site. Such striking and elegantly gathered results confirmed the previously listed predictions about the spread of bones and various types of artefact.

To summarize these results two generalizations appeared acceptable:–

1. Most unburnt and burnt bones, worked bones, and pottery occurred centrally and probably in association with hearths and to a lesser extent with houses (hearth locations did not entirely correspond with house locations).
2. Percentage prominence of the most common domestic species appeared graded from central to peripheral zones in order of increasing size of bones or increasing body size of animal species, e.g. Fig. 9. Thus larger bones predominated relatively abundantly at the periphery of the occupation site.

–0–

At this stage of investigation, examination of upper layers of occupation deposits had been limited so that few firm stratigraphic links could be made between the majority of bone detritus and particular types of structure on the site. Nevertheless sampling patterns comparable to the concentric pattern were constructed around the central points or squares of each type of site structure, namely the locations of houses, hearths and four post structures, for example see Fig. 10. Bone data within the grid system was regrouped according to these new quasi–concentric sampling templates and the results were examined.

Bones were found to be least associated with the four–post structures in the central area. This should not be surprising since these structures are commonly interpreted as built for grain storage and not for any animal related activities.

By contrast, Table 7 shows that bone debris was closely associated with the location of hearths and houses. While there was a noticeable concentration of bone debris at and around internal and external hearths, the majority of bones occurred closer to the centres of houses than to the hearths. Some 80% of bones lay within 14 m of the house centres; the greatest accumulations lay between 4 m and 7 m away from house centres, that is just outside where the walls had stood.

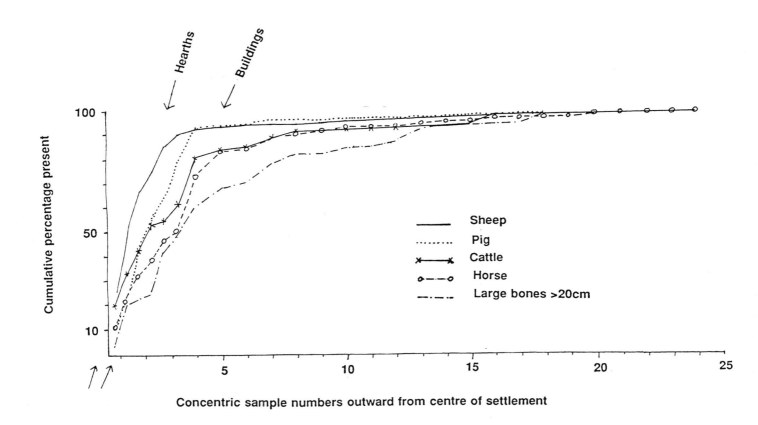

Fig. 9. Distribution of medium sized and large mammal and 'large' bones in the concentric sample area.

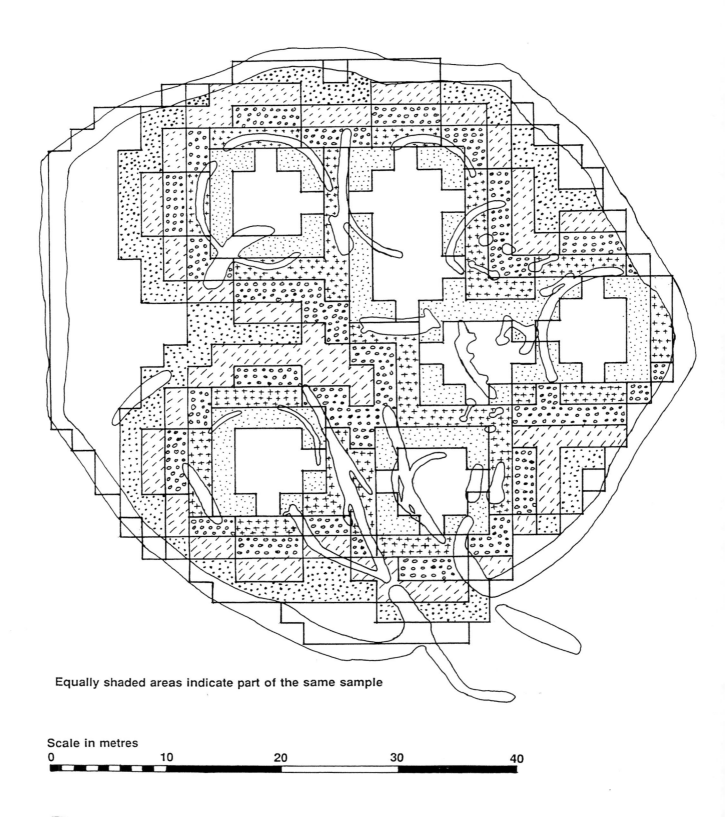

Equally shaded areas indicate part of the same sample

Scale in metres

| 0 | 10 | 20 | 30 | 40 |

Fig. 10. Quasi concentric sample template based on the centres of each of the buildings at Mingies Ditch (from Wilson 1993).

Beyond this patterning it appeared too difficult to unravel the detailed spread of site debris with individual houses or hearths. However, it was clear that the trends of general spreads of species and other bone debris around houses and hearths repeated most trends found in the overall concentric sampling of the site.

Bones appeared more closely clustered around hearths and houses than at the centre of the site although it was difficult to be certain whether bone–related activities were more associated with the centre of the site or whether they were associated with the houses and hearths which coincidentally happened to be located close to the centre of the site.

A plan of an abandoned Maasai village in Kenya recorded by Gifford and others offered a possible comparison (Ammerman, Gifford & Voorrips 1978, Fig.1). There bones lay around the crumbling houses and were less common in the central area. However, the Maasai houses surrounded a much larger central area than at Mingies Ditch. Since at both sites most bones appeared to have accumulated within 15 m of the houses, the simplest or most parsimonious conclusion was that the central accumulation of bones at Mingies Ditch was of coincidental occurrence and due to the proximity of the houses at an average of 14.5 m from the site centre.

Although Maasai and Celtic cultures must have their differences, from the ecocultural viewpoint differences in site activities may be less than supposed. If the map of the bone distribution at the Maasai village (Voorrips, Gifford & Ammerman 1978, Fig. 15.2), is examined, it is found that caprovine (sheep and goat) bones predominate where bones are most abundant while bovine (predominantly cattle) bones predominate where bone densities are low, a finding which parallels the relationship between species composition and density of bones at Mingies Ditch. In other words, it is not the exact species composition which is important in determining bone distributions at sites but the size of bones or the size of species individuals. Similar ecocultural activities appear to operate at sites occupied by communities of substantially different cultures.

Having presented the obvious trends of bone debris, more complex distributions are worth mentioning. Both cattle and dog skull debris appear to have bimodal distributions, such debris occurring away from houses and hearths and thus tending to accumulate peripherally and at the site centre. The following chapter accounts for such greater complexity.

–0–

An important issue should be discussed at this juncture. Having identified some fairly novel trends among site debris, it will be asked if these trends are authentic and not a product of site processes other than scavenging, rubbish clearance and butchery? In particular, are the concentric patterns of debris due to the high degree of bone degradation found at the site? These questions were discussed in a separate paper (Wilson 1985).

In preparing that work, it was clear that many elements and many epiphyses of animal skeletons at Mingies Ditch had been destroyed during the events of the last two thousand years. Bones of young individuals and of small and medium sized species had been more degraded than bones of older individuals and of the largest species.

To understand the spatial spread of degraded bones further, an index of bone degradation, based on the percentage of best surviving elements of sheep in the total number of surviving bones of sheep, was calculated for different sample groups from the site. It was shown by this index first that, as one would expect, bone degradation decreased with increasing depth of feature deposits below the ground surface.

Second, the degradation index indicated that bones from central areas of the site were more degraded than those from the site periphery. This made sense since the peripheral deposits of bones were generally buried deeper in the ground than those of centrally located deposits.

It was fortunate that bones of sheep and pig were abundant and their percentages were relatively high in the central area where degradation was greatest, for one would expect the more robust bones of cattle and horse to survive better and be represented by relatively high percentages but this did not occur. Conversely, the results meant that low percentages of sheep and pig where bone preservation was better were even more unlikely to be caused by bad preservation.

'It is therefore concluded that the concentric pattern of species data is mainly due to Iron Age human activity or contemporary scavenging by [other] *animals.'* (Wilson 1985, 90).

Table 7 Cumulative percentages of site debris at maximum radial distance of quasi concentric sample areas from the centres of different types of structure

a) Cumulative percentages inside and away from buildings

#	Max rad dist	Excav area %	Pot fabric A %	Pot fabric B %	Wkd bones %	Burnt bones black %	Burnt bones white %	Dog bns %	Sheep teeth' %	Pig teeth %	Cattle teeth %	Cattle all bones %	Horse teeth %	Horse all bns %	Large frags 10cm+ %	Large frags 20cm+ %
1	3.7	31.3	27	32	40	25	23	17	32	39	17	21	19	16	17	25
2	5.5	56.6	40	55	60	52	50	50	58	58	40	43	49	39	21	50
3	7.0	74.9	67	75	70	82	79	83	85	89	70	73	76	66	67	75
4	8.5	82.3	80	91	90	89	92	83	95	97	84	85	80	75	82	81
5	10.6	88.6	96	99	100	100	98	83	98	97	89	90	90	84	89	88
6	nc	94.8	99	100	100	100	100	100	99	98	95	94	92	86	91	88
7	nc	100	100	100	100	100	100	100	100	100	100	100	100	100	100	100

b) Cumulative percentages at and around hearths

#	Rad	Area	A	B	Wkd	black	white	Dog	Sheep	Pig	Cattle teeth	Cattle bns	Horse teeth	Horse bns	Large 10cm+	Large 20cm+
1	4.4	44.7	46	48	70	47	45	50	61	44	40	41	23	29	27	25
2	7.0	62.4	71	68	80	78	74	67	80	68	60	61	50	46	55	63
3	9.4	73.4	90	86	90	88	92	67	89	76	76	73	65	59	69	72
4	12.2	79.8	93	95	90	92	94	67	92	83	79	76	69	62	71	72
5	13.7	87.4	96	97	90	95	98	67	97	86	85	83	81	77	77	75
6	14.8	94.3	97	99	100	98	100	83	98	91	87	87	97	89	81	78
7	nc	100	100	100	100	100	100	100	100	100	100	100	100	100	100	100

c) Cumulative percentages at and around four post structures

#	Rad	Area	A	B	Wkd	black	white	Dog	Sheep	Pig	Cattle teeth	Cattle bns	Horse teeth	Horse bns	Large 10cm+	Large 20cm+
1	6.3	15.9	6	5	20	27	11	-	8	11	10	5	10	7	3	-
2	9.8	32.9	29	43	60	40	38	33	39	41	35	37	25	28	29	34
3	13.8	51.3	70	74	90	72	79	71	80	65	59	58	49	47	52	44
4	18.7	70.2	84	93	100	88	93	83	88	92	80	78	71	71	72	89
5	nc	87.3	98	99	100	100	99	100	98	100	90	87	80	81	85	88
6	nc	95.9	99	100	100	100	100	100	100	100	99	100	93	90	99	97
7	nc	100	100	100	100	100	100	100	100	100	100	100	100	100	100	100

' 'Teeth' include all loose and anchored teeth of a species.
From Wilson 1993.

Chapter 5

Interpreting and Explaining the Concentric or Radial Spreads of Bones at Mingies Ditch

Having concluded in Chapter 4 that the spatial patterning of Iron Age bones at Mingies Ditch was an authentic phenomenon indicative of ancient activities, it is useful to add that the patterning appeared similar in principle to that observed at Barton Court Farm although there was little evidence of any radial symmetry among the generally rectangular layout of features there. While some of the probable settlement processes contributing to spatial patterns have already been identified, a deeper discussion of their impact and interaction at Mingies Ditch is clearly important.

With the recognition that probably most site debris was associated with houses and hearths, it did not entirely follow that these structures were the sources of the bones which were found there. Explanatory emphasis had to rest most with the location of former site activities and less with the location of site structures. Bone locations might represent residual debris of bone dumps after other bones were moved or removed elsewhere, or they might represent accumulations of bones scattered and rescattered from other places.

Since typically the recovered debris was highly disarticulated and broken up, it would appear that most bones there were moved a number of times by destructive forces as well as by nondestructive ones. Some of the movement would appear random in creating fairly uniform spreads, such as of the bones largely of medium sized mammals centrally, but clearly some sorting processes had produced the central to peripheral zoning of species debris.

Although bones of medium sized mammals were subject to scattering processes, it appeared that it was the larger bones which were most subject to scattering by processes such as scavenging and rubbish clearance. Therefore spreads of smaller bone debris were more likely to indicate original domestic sources than scatters of larger bones, unless of course there was evidence of bones having been dumped directly at a location and not scattered thereafter. There was scarce evidence of the latter so it can be argued that the sheep and pig bones around houses and hearths at Mingies Ditch were representative of site activities in those locations before such species bones were broken and scattered. By and large the movements of bones from dumping places were part randomly spread and part outwardly directed.

Jumping to the simplest conclusion that there was only a differential radiation or an overall centrifugal (i.e. outward) 'drift' of bones, especially large ones, at Mingies Ditch may be highly tempting. However, it was expected that meat joints would have been brought from butchery places to hearths and houses for cooking and eating, implying an initial inward or centripetal movement of some bones from more peripheral sources to the vicinity of hearths and houses.

For the peripheral locations of butchery, it was inferred that other carcass bones may have been left at these peripheral sources and subjected to scattering from there. Thus in general the spatial spread of bones resulted from different activities in different parts of the site. From these sources and different processes moving bones there had been a great criss–crossing of invisible trajectories of bones over the site. In other words, the bone spread is a complicated phenomenon to explain.

–0–

It seemed best to start from the latest events and processes on site and work back to the preliminary ones. A complete list of contributory processes must include the effects of any excavation damage to bones, any factors of differential retrieval of bones from the soil, and, most importantly at Mingies Ditch, the short and long term degradation of bones by leaching and mechanical pressures such as the trampling of bones before and, in shallow deposits, after burial. As previously outlined, these destructive effects, however, were held to be minor components in the formation of the differentiated spatial pattern of bones described.

First one focussed on the scavenging of site refuse by domesticated and wild animals. One overall effect would be the breaking up of many bones into smaller fragments, many of which were destroyed in animal guts, surviving pieces defaecated, while other fragments were dropped where bones were gnawed, chewed and occasionally vomited (Payne & Munson 1985, also Binford 1981, 35–86) A related outcome was that scavenging disarticulates as well as fragments the elements of the skeleton. Articulated and whole bones were not common in the exposed spreads of debris and scavenging undoubtedly contributed to this.

The most important consideration was the distances and the directions that bones were moved. Domesticated scavengers would be unlikely to have carried bones far from the settlement since they would be rarely threatened or disturbed by human behaviour. Dogs may have been either tethered or relatively free to settle down close to houses and activity areas to gnaw and crush bones. Any competition between dogs might have led to a wider spread of debris (Payne pers. comm.). Wild or feral animal species probably carried some bones considerable distances, perhaps 50 m when one looks at the outermost locations of bones at the site. Scavenging birds must have lifted bones greater distances and outside the limits of excavation. Outside the settlement, a sparse, diffuse, and scarcely noticeable spread of bones would have lain slowly disintegrating in pasture and occasional scrub.

In general the movement of scavengers with bones would appear to have been a somewhat randomly outward direction from bone sources, animals making and spreading detritus over the settlement, particularly the central area, some bones being dropped in open spaces and against structures like houses, fences and the perimeter bank, and in refuges, other holes and ditches. Major scavengers like dogs, pigs and ravens would tend to have selected largest elements and fragments as supplies of marrow, gristle and meat shreds. Less enticing small, worked and burnt fragments would tend to have been ignored and left close to their original sources as the scavenging experiments have shown.

The next and *second* process of importance was rubbish disposal or clearance. At this site it was a reasonable assumption that bones and other rubbish were cleared from areas of intensive human action where they were a nuisance due to their various properties such as sharpness and bad odour and which could give aesthetic or symbolic offence or cause injuries. Initially we should consider occasional bones or loose scatters such as might accumulate through sporadic scavenging events or bones that had been kicked about by passing livestock. Then, we certainly should consider rubbish from food preparation and eating inside or out of houses. Detailed examination by Tim Allen of the stratigraphy and the low density of refuse in layers contemporary with house occupation indicates that meal rubbish was probably cleared out from houses but, to judge from the accumulation outside houses, probably was not carried far and was dumped fairly directly onto nearby ground. Remnants from food eaten outside might have been tossed aside carelessly or with some deliberation.

Larger skeletal elements, articulated bones and large fragments probably were the greatest nuisance and could cause accidents. Often they must have been removed, individually or collectively, away from areas of greatest human activity or social value, especially from domestic quarters, doorways, paths, hearths and places of status or sanctity. Any large bones were likely to have been quickly pushed or carried aside, thrown out to the settlement periphery, or occasionally into deeper features where there was a chance of burial.

In contrast, burnt and worked bones would probably be reduced in size (sawn or rounded off by working, made fragile by burning and broken by trampling), would receive little attention and would be less disturbed by rubbish clearance. This would help explain the persistence of such material at hearths and around houses.

By and large one has the impression of most surviving debris not travelling very far outside houses. There appears only to be a few metres between the occurrences of medium sized debris and coarser deposits. However this is only describing the residual, fairly quickly buried debris. And, in the central area there probably were many overlapping spreads of the two kinds of debris, in the main dominated by the presence of medium sized refuse.

Third and last, the next process of importance in the spatially patterned accumulation of Iron Age site debris was butchery and, particularly, the places of butchery are argued to be relevant. Primary fields of consideration involve the efficiency of butchery practices and other occupational activities affecting the spacing of butchery events. In talking of efficiency, it is not claimed that Iron Age culture and settlements were more efficient or more productive than other cultures, for example, Egyptian dynastic culture or 19th century industrial society. It is implicit in my discussion, however, that such anciently evolved practices as butchery and cooking should often operate with both economical and conservative constraints. These prehistoric and rural site activities are assumed to have attained a certain plateau of domestic efficiency but one which may well have been capable of improvement as the size, complexity and specialisation of occupations within societies increased, particularly in urban conditions.

The first consideration was that the area required for the slaughtering and butchery of a carcass was proportional to the size of the animal which was killed (see Fig. 1). And, the greater the area required, the greater the distance between the butchery site and the cooking place. Butchery of large animals like cattle would be displaced further than that of medium sized animals like sheep and more than small animals.

Cultural life, obviously, was more complicated than this simple relationship. Distance of displacement would be increased by the area required to carry out all functions of cooking at the hearth and any other necessary fireside or household activities. Even spatial aspects such as the handy storage of cooking vessels would displace butchery farther afield. Social custom and ritual values may have prescribed greater rather than smaller distances of displacement.

Consider, second, that the size of carcass broadly determined the extent and the type of butchery required. Large carcasses were likely to have been treated differently to small carcasses. This factor of carcass size influenced which bones of different species would be carried to the fire as part of meat joints or as part of whole (generally smaller) carcasses which were carried to the fire for cooking.

Small carcasses could be cooked quickly with a minimum of butchery and a small amount of firewood. Small carcasses bore limited amounts of meat which were not separated from the bone until eating.

Medium and large size carcasses had to be cut up for ease and economy of handling and cooking. Sizeable quantities of meat on medium sized carcasses, such as of sheep, indicate that butchery would require mainly a disjointing of the carcass. Most bones of sheep, however, might have been regarded as too small and awkward to be worth removing before cooking.

By contrast, the masses of meat on carcasses of cattle and other large species require cutting into suitable size pieces for cooking. Retainment of large bones in the meat to be cooked would be inconvenient and uneconomical although it is said they are good conductors of heat (Robinson pers. comm.). Here it is assumed that ox roasts, that is of the whole carcass or large parts of it, were not the cultural norm – not an unreasonable assumption for what is believed to have been a settlement existing at subsistence level (One must conceed, however, the possibility that some carcass parts including meat came from or were sent to other settlements).

Thus transport of bones in one form or other to cooking and eating areas would require the subsequent dispersal of at least the larger bones from such places. Large bones, however, would best be left at the site periphery by butchery before cooking. Thus more effort would go into the intensive butchery of large carcasses but at least less firewood would be required for cooking by the separation of meat from the skeleton.

If bones were needed for marrow then they were brought in to cook. They would be broken to obtain the marrow and the largest fragments no doubt would be cleared from cooking and eating areas.

Occasionally there might have been a gathering for a feast and the scale of operations would alter with more effort at gathering firewood for a large fire and perhaps larger portions of the carcass being cooked. Alternatively, the quantities of beef required and the manner of its presentation, perhaps more ostentatious, might still dictate the deboning of meat on the periphery of domestic or ritual areas.

As economic and ergonomic factors like those discussed intensified with carcass size, it became imperatively easier to separate the bones from the meat and to take only the meat, desired body organs and marrow bones to the fireside for cooking. The remainder of the skeleton and other waste like gut contents could have been left at the butchery site or dumped a short distance farther on the site periphery and with a minimum of effort.

All these factors should displace the butchery of large carcasses to the periphery of the domestic area or a wider occupation area. Nevertheless, lengthy distances from slaughtering and butchery places to hearths are not envisaged since the weight of the meat to be carried would be significant.

At Mingies Ditch the general spread of bones suggests that more carcass butchery occurred within 2 m and 10 m from the houses and hearths. This suggestion can scarcely be supported when it was impossible at this site to distinguish between groups of generally spread bones and groups of bones left over from the boning out of larger carcasses. Any articulated limb or body elements of cattle and horse left after butchery were too degraded by scavenging and subsequent processes to survive as evidence of butchery spatial location. Articulated bones of two piglets were found on the periphery of the occupation area but were difficult to relate to butchery location since the bones lacked butchery marks.

–0–

Interpretations and explanations discussed above are regarded as a general framework of basic factors which exerted much influence on the way cultures functioned in terms of butchery, cooking and eating at the simpler settlements. However, such human behaviour could have been modified further by other cultural preferences we can only guess at.

It is clear too that these essentially functionalist explanations are a response to the general spatial pattern of bone distribution as determined at Mingies Ditch. Actual site activities were a great deal more complicated as can be seen by the spatial variation of features in the site plan from the generalities described. In addition the interpretation of site features in the other functioning and longer term development of the settlement as given in the main report (Allen & Robinson 1993) may not strike many chords of agreement with my general account (Wilson 1993).

Hints of such complexity occur with the bimodal distributions of cattle and dog skull debris which could suggest that dog carcasses were disposed of whole, hence the association of their relatively small bones with some larger ones of cattle. Further examples of bones indicating more complicated activities were three teeth of beaver and two pieces of human skull which had even more distant 'peripheral' distributions than the bones of the large domesticated animals. The spread of beaver teeth contradicts the species size trend but it appears that two of the teeth did not belong to the period of the main settlement occupation and therefore were related to locations and activities somewhat different to those discussed. Human bones at other Iron Age settlements have already been described as having peripheral locations (Whimster 1981 and C. Wilson 1981) but there is insufficient evidence here to discuss the significance of this phenomenon further.

–0–

Our greatest gain from this excavation was the quantification of ordinary bone data in a manner that fairly convincingly mapped and summarised the spatial spread of bones by simple if time–consuming methods. This demonstrated the great detrital variation of bones on the site and in relation to particular site structures. Gratifyingly, the results confirmed some of the general trends indicated at Barton Court Farm although the site was unsuited for addressing the original anomaly observed in pit versus ditch contrasts. However other feature type variation in species bone distribution was documented.

Poor preservation of bones limited the extent of investigation, especially into skeletal element analysis and aspects of butchery, ageing and sexing of bones etc. Despite these drawbacks, it could be concluded that pottery, burnt and worked bones and the bones of sheep and pigs were most associated with domestic or household activity. Therefore the location of such debris at future sites could reasonably be taken as a good indicator of domestic activity, at least on Iron Age and Roman sites.

Chapter 6

A Challenge to Spatial Theory and the Elaboration of Butchery within the Model: Excavations at Mount Farm

After the bone collection from Mingies Ditch was analysed and reported, bones from Mount Farm, Berinsfield, near Dorchester on Thames, were examined. At the latter excavation, directed by George Lambrick, much soil was sieved by employees in wintry conditions during 1977 and 1978 (Lambrick 1978, 1979 and unpublished a).

Spatial information was not especially revealing despite widespread excavation and salvage. Apart from the rectangular lines of Roman field ditches, the disparate features lacked the symmetry and coherence of the settlement layouts at Mingies Ditch and Barton Court Farm – a plan of major features is provided in Fig. 11. Yet this rescue work and sieving research (Jones 1978) turned up new pieces of detail and fields of evidence for the analytical jigsaw of investigating Thames gravel sites.

Some pertinent results are given in Table 8. Iron Age debris from the pits and gullies near a possible house in the northern area of the site resembled the pattern of predominant sheep and pig bones around the houses and hearths at Mingies Ditch and in the pit groups and house gullies from Ashville, Appleford and Barton Court Farm. In the southern area, however, bones from the pits were more substantially of cattle and horse. The contrast of the large species bones from the pits with those elsewhere was emphasised by the prominence of crania and articulated vertebrae and limb bones, especially in two pits (Fs 652 and 671) – e.g. Fig. 12, in the adjoining Romano–British field ditches and in waterholes of both periods. Results from soil sieving controls indicated that the species percentage differences between bone groups from southern and northern areas were genuine.

Table 8 Percentages of bone fragment frequency according to feature type at Mount Farm, Berinsfield, Oxfordshire

Period	Pits Early Iron Age	Early Iron Age	Mid-late IA	Roman	Waterholes or wells Early IA	Mid IA	Roman	Saxon
North/South area of site	N	S	'S'	N+S	N+S	S	S	N
Fragment number	253	241	61	58	150	89	336	111
	%	%	%	%	%	%	%	%
Sheep/goat	52	25	48	48	16	28	18	18
Cattle	34	61	39	41	65	57	57	70
Pig	9	6	8	9	5	2	6	5
Horse	3	6	5	2	13	12	18	7
Dog	1	2	–	–	1	–	1	–

Period	Ditches(d) and gullies(g) Bronze Age	MIA	MIA	MIA	Roman	Saxon
North/South area	N	N	N	S	N	S
Fragment number	54	153	233	249	303	331
	d	house g	d	d	d/g	d
	%	%	%	%	%	%
Sheep/goat	15	35	45	47	36	37
Cattle	80	49	36	36	38	48
Pig	1	7	12	8	15	7
Horse	–	8	5	8	11	7
Dog	4	1	2	1	1	2

From Wilson unpublished a.

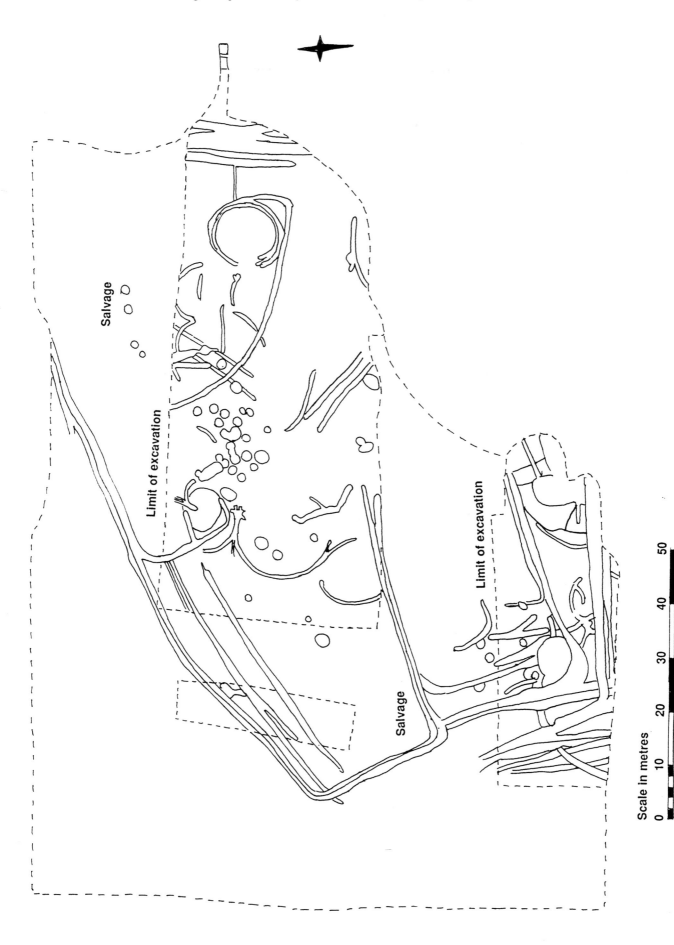

Fig. 11. Plan of Iron Age and Romano–British features at Mount Farm, Berinsfield (after Lambrick 1979).

From the widespread occurrence of articulated bones in the southern area during the Iron Age and Roman periods, it appeared that the butchery pattern of large carcasses was very similar over half a millenium of occupation. Thus the bones from this area are probably typical waste from rural Iron Age and Romano–British butchery. This point is emphasised as there has been discussion whether the cranial and articulated debris in Iron Age pits is indicative of Celtic ritual and exceptional rather than typical of sites, notably Danebury hillfort, Hampshire (Grant 1984, Cunliffe 1992 and Wilson 1992).

Normal butchery of large carcasses appears to have left complete and articulated bones and skulls on the ground surface at Mount Farm (in the fashion shown by Fig. 1), bones which were sometimes quickly disposed of and therefore well preserved by jumbled burial in deeper features. Comparable remains of sheep and pig in the same area were virtually absent. Thus these remains fitted what would be predicted of a peripheral area some 5 m – 15 m or more from hearths or house centres at Mingies Ditch. Unfortunately for verification, such structures were not identified in the southern area and it could not be ascertained whether or not they had lain in the adjoining area which was deeply quarried or badly disturbed by earthmoving machinery.

It is conceivable that the waterholes influenced the location of butchery, for example allowing the washing or steeping of carcass products like skins or guts. Possibly meat was carried 90 m to the most obvious house. It is more probable, however, that beasts were slaughtered close to where the bulk of meat was to be consumed, i.e. close to houses and hearths, so it would be carcass products other than meat which were carried to the waterholes.

–0–

Articulated bones from Mount Farm helped to confirm the suspected form of Iron Age butchery of large carcasses, e.g. Fig. 13. A description of this butchery enables a better understanding of where it took place and indicates any specific skeletal evidence which helps to identify slaughtering places.

At Ashville the lack of evidence for dividing carcasses into equal halves indicated that the bodies of cattle and horse were not hung up for butchery. Occasional sheep and horse skeletons lacking front limbs at Ashville (F82) and Farmoor (F37) (Wilson 1978b and 1979) and disarticulated limbs at Ashville, Barton Court and Mount Farm confirm that limbs were probably removed from the carcass by cutting under the shoulder blade and through the pelvis or femur as the carcass lay on the ground after skinning. Articulated skulls and backbones of cattle and horse at these sites and others (Wilson unpub. a) indicate that meat was then stripped from the large portions of the skeleton before cooking. Often, for convenience or communal sharing, the backbone was chopped into sections and the head detached from the neck as shown by complete skulls and articulated vertebrae from City Farm, Hanborough, Oxfordshire, Mount Farm and

Barton Court Farm (again it is worth referring to Fig. 1 but bearing in mind differences between hunter–gatherers and pastoral Celtic husbandries). No charring of articulated bones has been recorded to indicate that whole limbs were roasted although one end of a section of horse backbone from pit F652 at Mount Farm was charred and may either have been roasted or accidentally burnt.

As evidence of meat stripping from the skeleton and meat joints, knife cuts and certain breaks are found on articulated and loose Iron Age bones, Fig. 14. Chop marks are most common on Romano–British ones as shown recently by comprehensive butchery records from Claydon Pike, Fairford, Gloucestershire, Fig. 15 (Wilson & Levitan unpub.). Especially for cattle, chopping and trimming is unmistakeable downwards and sometimes up the sides of upper limb bones and into awkward joints, particularly the hock joint. Slivers of bone were sliced off with the beef. All this suggests rapid butchery carried out while many bones were still articulated.

Meat trimming along the backbone took place from anterior and posterior directions but it is occasionally noticeable that where the sacrum of cattle was trimmed off, this happened from the front. This is opposite the effect of downward halving of carcasses hung by the backlegs as occurs in modern butchery. The idea that prehistoric and Romano–British carcass division took place on or close to the ground therefore gains greater credibility. Further evidence of this is that head removal often occurred from the underside of the carcass but this evidence is not incontrovertible.

Some smaller carcases may have been hung for butchery. A sheep skeleton of possible Roman date at Farmoor (Wilson 1979) was cut down through the sacrum close to the midline but most rural site evidence points to butchery on the ground, a chopping block or low table.

If butchery of carcasses took place at a low level in the absence of suitably strong structures on which to hoist large carcases, there is less reason to expect that any single slaughtering spot should be persisted with. Small carcases could, however, be hung from a number of unspecialised structures. Thus butchery probably occurred at convenient distance from other site activities and the gradually changing locations of houses, hearths, other structures and waterholes. Random variation in the location of slaughtering spots would be normal but approximating within the broad confines of functional efficiency already discussed.

Such carcass treatment at farmstead sites is also likely to have been undertaken by earlier prehistoric mobile societies. However, the form of rural butchery was transformed at settlements of increasing size and different spatial organisation, namely Iron Age oppida, and later at Roman, Saxon and medieval towns, forts and castles (chapter 11).

Rural butchery like that envisaged at Mount Farm has archaeological consequences. If most beef was removed from bones at the slaughtering place, then most skeletal elements would tend to be dumped together close by.

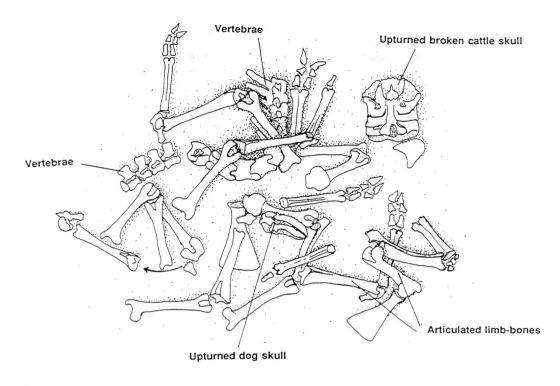

Fig. 12. Articulated bones and crania at the bottom of Iron Age pit F652 at Mount Farm.

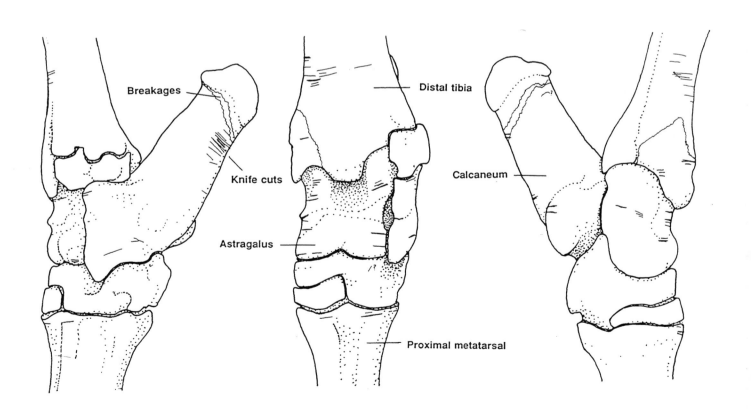

Fig. 13. Butchery knife cuts and breakages on the bones of the hock joint of cattle as found on articulated bones in Pit F652.

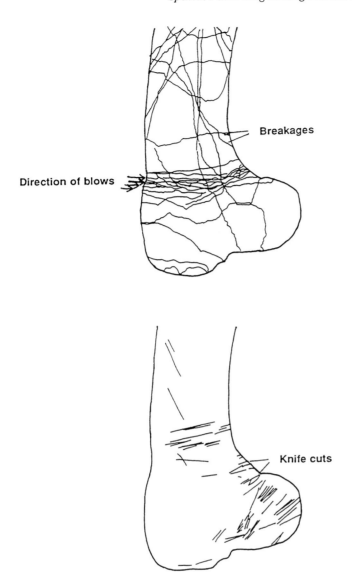

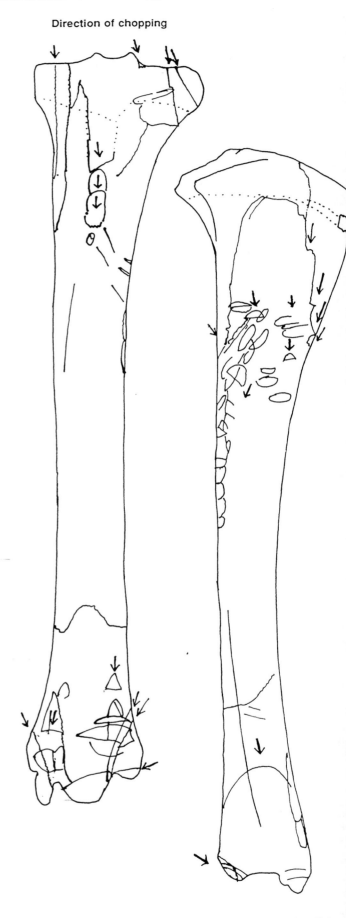

Direction of chopping

Breakages

Direction of blows

Knife cuts

Fig. 14. Butchery knife cuts and breakages on the medial aspect of the humerus of Iron Age cattle as recorded at Ashville Trading Estate, Abingdon (Wilson 1978b).

Fig. 15. Butchery marks, chiefly trimming scars, on the anterior and medial aspects of the tibia of Romano–British cattle as recorded at Claydon Pike, Fairford.

Frequencies of different skeletal elements would resemble their natural abundance in cattle and horse skeletons and probably would be indistinguishable from element frequencies of other accumulations of bones of the same species. Similarly, where the bones and butchery of smaller animals were considered, most skeletal elements of the carcass would end up as a mixed accumulation although, distributed through cooking, eating and refuse dumping processes near hearths and houses, it would tend to be a different place to that of bones of large carcasses.

Inspection of the skeletal element distributions of Iron Age and Roman rural groups has usually failed to yield clues to carcass butchery and butchery places but this is now not surprising considering the argument and description of butchery above. One conspicuous skeletal exception to the rule of nondescript skeletal composition at rural sites is a cluster of cattle horn cores found in a Romano–British building at Kingston Bagpuize, Oxfordshire (Wilson 1976). Comparable deposits are found in Roman towns such as Camulodunum, Exeter, London and Silchester. This reflects the greater craft and semi–industrial concerns of cities rather than the countryside although raw material for horn or leather working or other crafts may have been collected and worked on a small scale at small settlements in the countryside. Thus such horn core groups are indicative of the location of skin treatment places if not of slaughtering places.

These aspects of butchery should be considered when taking account of the demonstrated spatial patterning of prehistoric and Romano–British settlement bones.

Chapter 7

A Bone Expert's Dream: the Medieval Manor at Hardings Field

After Mount Farm the next excavation collection of bones in the Upper Thames Valley to promise useful information on spatial arrangement of site activities was from the 13th to 15th century A.D. moated manor of Hardings Field, Chalgrove, Oxfordshire. Philip Page and Richard Chambers directed excavations over several seasons during 1977 to 1979 and revealed substantial stone and other foundations of buildings and a farmyard (Chambers 1978 and Page 1979, 1980, 1982, 1983 and unpub.). An illustration of the reconstructed manorhouse is given by Fig. 16.

First impression of the site layout of the manor farmyard discloses two similarities with the site layout at Mingies Ditch. Manor buildings were enclosed by a stream entering a moat of uncertain function, scarcely investigated but superficially comparable to the enclosure ditches and stream channel at the Iron Age site. In both settlements the buildings surrounded a central area. There the structural similarities end.

At Mingies Ditch the Iron Age buildings appeared typically

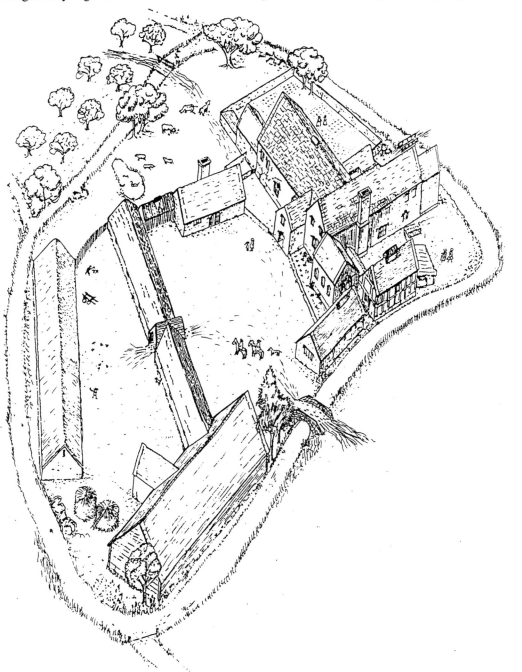

Fig. 16. Reconstruction drawing of the manor house at Hardings Field, Chalgrove (after M. Aston in Page 1983).

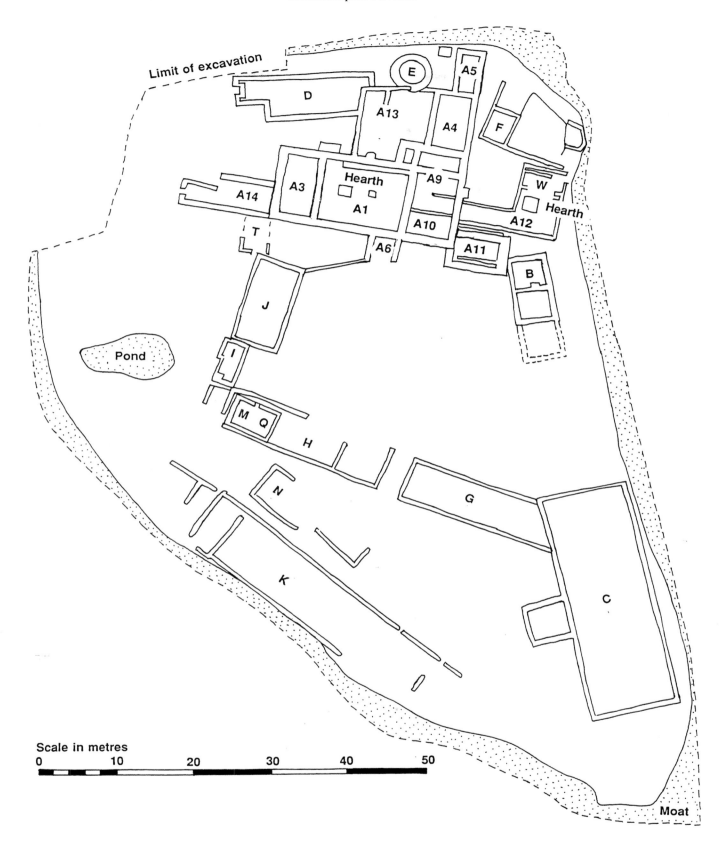

Fig. 17. Plan of the buildings and the yards of the manor at Hardings Field (from Page 1979).

to be simple rural houses of similar modest size and conical shape, one or two of which stood within the enclosure at any one time. Each house was probably the single and complete nucleus of animal management and household activity. By contrast, the medieval manor buildings were variable in size, rectagular shape, aggregation and symmetry. These buildings also altered in form over several centuries and at each phase showed a marked and elaborate structural division of farmyard and living quarters corresponding to the complex functions of an arable manor.

Preliminary examination of a small site sample of bones took place in 1980. Soon it was obvious that the bones were not heavily degraded by leaching and other destruction within the soil. Bones of fish, bird and small mammals were to be commonly found in many deposits.

Serious work on the bones did not begin until 1983. Research proposals focussed on the comparison of bone distributions in and around the building foundations.

Most bone debris was excavated from the vicinity of the main group of buildings known collectively as Block A, and in particular within individual rooms numbered A1, A9, and A10, Fig. 17. This concentration of debris could reflect some bias in the focus of excavation but this appears immaterial since two impressive groups of evidence showed that the spatial patterning of debris was comparable and broadly similar to that found at Mingies Ditch and Barton Court Farm.

First, bones from deposits inside the buildings contained high percentages of elements from sheep and pig, small mammals like rabbit and hare, birds such as domestic fowl and goose, and marine and freshwater fish. Bone collections from outside the buildings had a greater abundance of cattle and horse. In other words, internal deposits consisted of relatively small and fine debris while that from external deposits was of a larger and coarser kind, Table 9.

Second, bone debris from the various rooms and buildings

Table 9 Percentage comparisons of bones and shells in internal and external contexts of buildings at Hardings Field manor, Chalgrove.

| Phase | Internal contexts | | | | | | | External contexts | | | | |
	1	2	3/1	3/2 & 3/3	4/2	5	All phases	2	3/1	4/2	5	All phases
% of identification	50	32	29	19	25	31	28.1	38	39	48	33	36.7
% of burnt bones	–	–	1	–	1	+	0.5	1	–	–	+	0.3
Total of cattle, horse, pig&sheep(n)	12	79	177	22	342	380	1134	139	68	348	913	1468
% of sheep	17	6	23	36	21	28	22.8	18	29	18	23	21.3
% of pig	67	65	49	50	56	34	46.4	31	28	39	33	34.1
% of cattle	8	28	28	14	22	36	29.6	45	42	43	43	43.3
% of horse	8	1	1	–	+	2	1.2	6	–	–	1	1.3
Index %s of n Deer	–	–	1	–	1	2	1.4	2	2	1	1	1.4
Dog	–	–	2	–	1	1	0.9	2	2	1	1	1.0
Cat	–	2	–	–	+	1	1.0	1	–	1	1	0.5
Rabbit & hare	8	5	6	5	8	7	6.5	–	–	1	4	2.8
Rodent	–	4	1	–	5	34	13.8	–	2	+	4	2.4
Domestic fowl	50	3	47	59	70	60	50.4	7	–	6	15	11.5
Domestic goose	–	3	51	23	19	21	21.1	5	3	1	5	4.0
Other bird	25	5	65	232	76	61	26.6	3	3	9	14	11.0
Fish	8	–	6	–	59	23	26.6	1	–	+	1	1.0
Oyster	17	8	69	46	88	107	79.3	19	19	54	92	72.3
Mussel	–	15	4	–	21	27	17.3	26	–	+	3	4.3

From Wilson 1989a.

Table 10 Percentage comparisons of bones and shells in buildings and rooms at Hardings Field manor

Buildings/Room number	A 1	A 3	A 4	A 5	A 6	A 9	A 10	A 11	A 12	A 13	A 14	B	D	F	G	H	I	J	K	M	P	Q	R	T	W
% of identification	14	25	29	39	100	22	27	67	34	29	75	31	44	27	49	33	100	30	24	33	80	29	100	34	37
% of burnt bones	0.3	-	-	-	-	0.1	-	-	0.3	5.9	-	-	-	22	-	-	-	-	-	33	-	-	-	1.7	-
Total of cattle, horse, pig & sheep	87	18	45	210	1	180	41	10	247	10	15	51	8	75	23	35	-	7	4	1	5	2	3	20	31
% cattle & horse	15	17	33	40	100	17	15	60	31	30	13	47	38	45	30	43	-	43	50	100	20	50	-	20	33
% sheep & pig	85	83	67	60	-	83	85	40	69	70	87	53	62	55	70	57	-	57	50	-	80	50	100	80	77
Index % of:-																									
Deer	-	-	-	1.4	-	0.6	-	10	2	-	13	4	-	0.3	-	-	-	-	-	-	-	-	-	-	-
Dog	-	-	-	1.0	-	0.6	-	-	0.4	-	-	2	-	4.0	-	-	>100	1.4	-	-	-	-	-	-	-
Cat	2.3	-	-	3.8	-	-	-	-	-	-	-	-	-	2.9	-	-	-	-	-	-	-	-	-	-	-
Rabbit & hare	11.5	-	2.2	2.4	-	12.8	17.1	-	5.7	-	6.7	2.0	-	4.0	-	5.7	-	-	-	-	20	-	-	-	6.5
Rodent	3.4	28	-	60	-	3.3	-	-	3.6	-	-	5.9	13	-	-	-	-	-	-	-	-	-	-	-	-
Domestic fowl	82	11.1	56	11.4	-	172	105	-	30	10	40	9.8	13	12	-	26	>800	-	-	-	-	-	-	5	16
Domestic goose	21	22	24	8.1	-	52	137	-	15	-	27	9.8	13	5.3	-	-	>100	-	-	-	-	-	-	-	9.7
Other bird	199	61	38	27	-	132	188	-	31	-	20	7.8	-	20	4.3	5.7	-	-	-	-	-	-	-	-	13
Fish	132	-	-	5.7	-	87	34	-	2.4	-	13	2.0	-	4.0	-	-	>500	-	-	-	-	-	-	-	-
Oyster	117	-	40	33	-	286	29	100	30	60	53	22	13	31	-	17	>100	29	25	-	-	50	33	135	19
Mussel	17	21	-	3	-	62	44	10	13	-	7	-	-	1	-	3	-	-	-	-	-	-	-	-	-

From Wilson 1989a.

Table 11 **Rank order of frequencies, percentages and percentage indicies given in Tables 9 and 10 in order to determine the rooms or buildings most associated with cooking and eating**

Building/Room	A 1	A 3	A 4	A 5	A 6	A 9	A 10	A 11	A 12	A 13	A 14	B	D	F	G	H	I	J	K	L	P	Q	R	T	W
No. of bones Highest = 1	3	11	8	4	24	1	7	19	2	14	16	6	17	5	13	9	24	15	18	22	21	20	22	12	10
% identified Lowest = 1	1	4	7	17	23	2	5	20	14	7	21	11	18	5	19	12	23	10	3	12	22	7	13	14	16
% burnt Highest = 1	5	8	8	8	8	7	8	8	5	2	8	8	8	3	8	8	8	8	8	1	8	8	3	4	8
% sheep&pig Highest = 1	3	5	13	15	23	5	3	22	12	10	2	19	14	18	10	16	23	16	20	23	7	20	1	7	9
% rabbit&hare	4	13	11	10	13	3	2	13	7	13	5	12	13	9	13	7	13	13	13	1	13	13	13	13	6
% dom. fowl	4	12	5	12	17	2	3	17	9	14	6	15	10	11	17	8	1	17	17	17	17	17	17	16	9
% dom. goose	7	6	5	12	14	3	1	14	8	14	4	10	9	13	14	14	2	14	14	14	14	14	14	14	11
% fish	1	9	9	5	9	2	3	9	7	9	4	8	9	6	9	9	9	9	9	9	9	9	9	9	9
% oyster	3	20	7	9	20	1	13	4	12	5	6	16	19	11	20	8	20	13	15	20	20	7	9	2	17
Sum of rankings	31	88	73	92	151	26	45	126	76	88	72	105	117	81	113	91	123	115	117	131	119	115	116	91	95
Order of ranking totals	2	8	5	12	25	1	3	23	6	8	4	14	19	7	15	10	22	16	19	24	21	16	18	10	13

Rank order of rooms or buildings most associated with cooking and eating:-
A9, A1, A10, A14, A4, A12, F, A3, A13, H, T, A5, W, B, J, Q, R, D, K, P, I, A11, M, A6.

From Wilson 1989a.

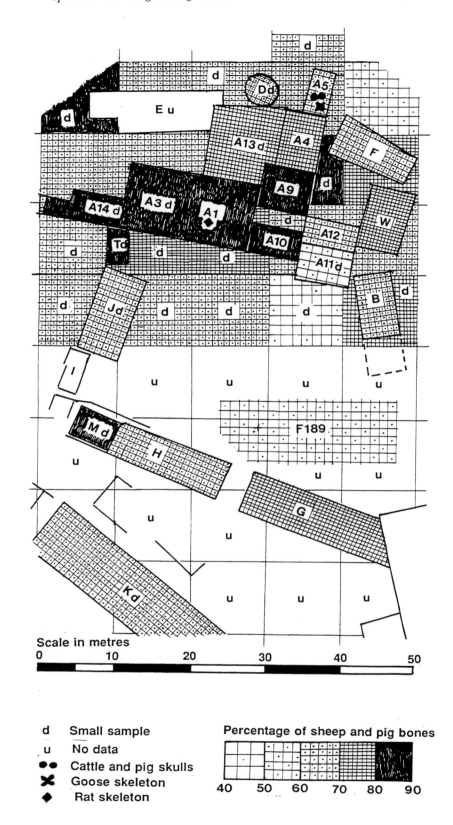

Scale in metres

| 0 | 10 | 20 | 30 | 40 | 50 |

d   Small sample
u   No data
●●   Cattle and pig skulls
✖   Goose skeleton
◆   Rat skeleton

Percentage of sheep and pig bones

| 40 | 50 | 60 | 70 | 80 | 90 |

Fig. 18. Distribution of the medium sized debris at Hardings Field based on the percentages of sheep and pig bones in the totals of the four main species in each area.

was ranked by percentage indicies of the approximate size of individual species or of their bony remains, that is by the coarseness and fineness of bones and their fragments, Tables 10 and 11. Concentrations of the finest debris lay in Rooms A1, A9 and A10. Where the density of bones per area of building was crudely calculated, the densest deposits lay in the rooms listed above (Wilson unpub. b). Buildings further away yielded fewer, less dense and coarse bones. Fig. 18 shows the distribution of medium fine debris on the site. A few samples of sieved bones from the moat and buildings indicated that the pattern was a genuine one and not due to the bias of recovering fewer small bones from deposits outside the manor house. In the samples fish bones were much more abundant in Room A9 than in the moat, Table 12.

–0–

It has been stated that the manor bones are quite well preserved and any effects of leaching and other destructive processes in the soil and on excavation were unimportant in explaining the distribution of coarse and fine debris. However, the approximate index of bone degradation obtained from the elemental composition of the sheep bones did suggest that bones from outside the buildings were more degraded by a combination of butchery, scavenging, trampling and other processes than those bones in floor layers and in other internal features. Bearing in mind the species bone distribution at Mingies Ditch and the conclusion there that high levels of bone degradation did not make the

Table 12 Comparison of general types of bone debris recovered by sieving of external deposits from the moat and internal deposits from Room A9

Phase	Moat 2		Room A9 4-5	
	f	%	f	%
Coarse debris	2	2	–	–
Medium fine	4	4	17	1.7
Hare/rabbit	2	2	2	0.2
Unidentified mammal	66	69	438	43.9
All bird	17	18	227	22.8
Fish	4	4	314	31.5
Total	95		998	

From Wilson unpublished b.

In terms of feature type, floor and other occupation levels contained the smallest and finest debris. Coarser material occurred in the robbed wall trenches and the demolition levels above the floors. Almost no pits occurred on the site. Thus the observed bone distributions at the manor and at Iron Age and Roman sites appeared to occur almost independently of the type of feature involved and more according to the location of site activity, especially domestic activity.

At Mingies Ditch the remnants of medium sized species and burnt and worked bones were considered to be the best indicators of domestic activity. The same was assumed to be true of the debris at Hardings Field and therefore Rooms A9, A1, A10 and A14 were deduced to be the broad central focus of cooking and eating of food. Arguing independently from architectural and historical evidence, Philip Page arrived at the same identification of the domestic quarters. This verification gave greater confidence to the theoretical interpretation of site refuse at Mingies Ditch and most importantly to the soundness of the general principles of site interpretation.

species data too unreliable, it appeared that, at most, differential preservation altered results but did not substantially explain the patterning of bones observed at the manor.

Thus, consistent with the general interpretation of spatial patterns at Mingies Ditch and elsewhere, processes of scavenging, rubbish disposal and butchery are held to largely explain the spread of medieval debris. Happily, the better preservation of skeletal elements allowed an improved insight into two of the three main processes which produced the spatial pattern. Of the third process, scavenging, little further can be added about it except the supposition that its effect on spatial patterning was fairly constant at rural sites of different period. Dog, the best known scavenging species, appears abundant at all farming sites.

On the other hand, much greater variation was expected in the culturally influenced processes of butchery, cooking and rubbish disposal. Aspects of these will be examined at length in the following chapter.

The differential distribution of smaller and larger species bones outward was paralleled by distinctive trends in the percentages of skeletal elements from the head, feet and body of the medium and small sized species but not obviously of cattle. Tables 13 to 16 show the distribution patterns of skeletal elements of sheep, pig, rabbit, hare and domestic fowl in the most important deposits within rooms and buildings and where found in external feature contexts.

Elements of the body or main meat carcass of sheep, particularly vertebrae, were best represented in the deposits of Rooms A9, A10 and A1 and less well in other rooms, buildings and external feature groups, where head and foot bone were more common. Among pig bones, elements from the head, especially loose teeth, were abundant in most deposits, those of the body were also quite evenly spread, but deposits in Room A9, and to a lesser extent in Room A10, markedly differed in the high percentage of foot elements present, especially the metacarpals and metatarsals. Small samples of rabbit and hare and domestic fowl bones indicated a high percentage of body elements in deposits centred on Room A9 and a higher percentage of the feet and head elements farther away.

The significance of these results too will be dealt with in the following chapter.

Table 13 **Percentages of grouped skeletal elements of sheep from selected feature groups**

Room/buildgs/ features	Internal contexts							External features					
	A9	A10	A12	A1	A5	BFW	G-K	Moat upcast	Ct. yd	Destruct. F186	F189	Dump F573	Ctyd F578
Phase	3-5	3	4-5	2-5	2-5	3-5	3-5	2	4/2	5	5	5	5
No. of bones	30	9	58	27	21	45	20	19	30	78	28	15	31
	%	%	%	%	%	%	%	%	%	%	%	%	%
Head	4	22	19	11	29	33	50	16	17	27	29	33	19
Foot	13	–	10	11	19	13	15	11	10	19	7	20	10
Body	83	78	71	78	52	53	35	74	73	54	64	47	71
Mandible	3	–	9	4	10	13	10	–	10	8	18	13	10
Loose teeth	–	22	7	–	5	7	30	11	3	13	7	13	3
Vertebrae	43	22	12	11	5	4	–	5	–	5	11	7	10
Small bones	7	–	5	7	–	11	–	–	–	3	4	–	3
Metapodials	7	–	5	4	19	2	15	11	10	17	4	20	3
% index of degradation[1]	20	40	48	33	24	51	65	58	63	42	54	60	45

[1] = Percentage of loose teeth and fragments of mandible, tibia and radius
From Wilson 1989a.

Table 14 **Percentages of grouped skeletal elements of pig from selected feature groups**

Room/buildgs/ feature	Internal contexts						External contexts		
	A9	A10	A12	A1	BFW	G-K	F573	F189	F578
Phase	3-5	3-5	4/2	2-5	3-5	3/5	4/2	5	5
No. of bones	113	22	85	45	42	11	34	35	36
	%	%	%	%	%	%	%	%	%
Head	26	41	59	56	55	64	60	46	28
Foot	44	23	11	11	12	9	3	11	14
Body	30	36	31	33	33	27	47	43	58
Mandible	4	5	15	11	24	18	18	9	14
Loose teeth	14	32	27	33	26	27	9	26	11
Vertebrae	9	9	6	7	10	–	3	9	6
Small bones	12	9	7	9	5	9	3	6	–
Metapodials	32	14	4	2	7	–	–	6	14

From Wilson 1989a.

Table 15 Percentages of grouped skeletal elements
of rabbit and hare from selected feature groups

	Internal contexts				External contexts
Room/feature	A9	A10	A12	A1	573&189
Phase	3-5	3-5	4-5	2-5	4-5
No. of bones	23	7	15	12	9
	%	%	%	%	%
Head	-	-	-	8	11
Foot	-	29	-	17	33
Body	100	71	100	75	56
Mandible	-	-	-	-	11
Loose teeth	-	-	-	8	-
Vertebrae	26	14	-	8	11
Small bones	-	14	-	-	-
Metapodials	-	29	-	8	33

From Wilson 1989a.

Table 16 Percentages of grouped skeletal elements of
domestic fowl from selected feature groups

Room/feature	A9	A12	A1	A5	F186	F189	F504 & 508
Phase	3-5	4-5	2-5	3-5	5	5	5
No. of bones	289	74	43	24	41	15	27
	%	%	%	%	%	%	%
Head	-	-	-	4	-	-	-
Foot[1]	5	8	7	13	15	13	22
Body[2]	95	92	93	83	85	87	78

[1] = Tarsometatarsus and phalanges
[2] = Excluding ribs
From Wilson 1989a.

Chapter 8

Culturally Variable Explanations of Bone Spacing at the Manor

Chapter 7 dealt with the basic patterning of bone distribution at the manor of Hardings Field, compared this briefly with Mingies Ditch and other sites, and introduced similar broad ways of interpreting it. Here interpretation and explanation are continued, allowing that greater variation of explanation should be expected in discussing the culturally influenced practices of butchery, cooking and rubbish disposal at the manor.

The variation in the element distributions of different species described already required distinctions to be drawn about the extent to which butchery and rubbish disposal acted on the bones.

Differential rubbish disposal from buildings of the different sized bones and fragments might have produced the correlated patterns of species and element representation. Large bones of cattle would be most affected by rubbish clearance but, of all the major species in the building deposits, cattle were least well represented and no element distributional differences were detectable among their bones. This suggests either, that rubbish clearance from the manor buildings was fairly complete, or that very few cattle bones were normally part of domestic activities and were not usually present to require disposal. The first alternative may be true but here seems of less importance than the second, the significance of which is made clear by discussion of the nature of cattle butchery in chapter 6.

What was relevant was that the relatively small quantities of cattle bones found in the rooms of Block A appeared present largely as randomly accumulated debris originating from other sources. Supporting evidence of incidental inclusion of bones into these deposits was a pelvis and a penis bone of dog and which normally would be expected to have been articulated or at least deposited with other bones of dog. This explanation, by the random incorporation of some bones into the room deposits, cannot be applied to the accumulation and pattern of most of the smaller and finer debris there.

Where rubbish clearance is considered as the mechanism which created the accumulation of fine debris left over, it may well explain the overall species distribution but appears less plausible as the cause of the varied element distribution.

For the bones of the medium sized species, many of the largest elements, such as the limb bones, which were potentially available from the carcass for disposal, would already have been rendered smaller by previous butchery of the joints and further disjointing and breakage during the eating of meat at the table. This implied that any differential disposal by fragment size differences of this more homogeneous and somewhat smaller material was not as great as might have been at first supposed. By comparison, however, any cattle bones present would often be sizeable enough to attract attention and disposal.

When it came to explaining the scanty distribution of the small elements of the paws and the larger ones of the limb bones of rabbit and hare, exceptionally it was seen that bone size differences alone did not bring about the outward movement of larger bones. Since rabbits and hares are conspicuously smaller than cattle and sheep, their element and fragment sizes were insignificantly different compared with the bone size variations of the larger mammals. Equally important, the relative absence of small metapodial elements in deposits inside the buildings, and especially Room A9, can not be explained by a failure to recover them when so many small and fine bones of fish and birds were found there.

These considerations suggest that even though rubbish clearance from the buildings occurred to some extent, especially with the large bones, this factor is not sufficient to explain the variation between elements found for some species within the buildings and between internal and external contexts. In passing, similar reasoning, particularly from the reversal of expected size differences among rabbit and hare bones, tends also to exclude scavenging as a sufficient cause.

Since it was principally the distributions of elements of the medium and small sized species which were patterned, both rubbish clearance and scavenging appear implicated less and only the third group of causative factors was left to discuss, namely butchery practices. Differences in the type and place of butchery of the species must have been involved as concomitants of size differences of bones and the original carcasses.

Because cranial and foot elements of sheep were less common and body elements, especially vertebrae, were most frequent at the centre of the fine refuse, most of the sheep bones there in the rooms may have been derived from carcasses which had the feet and heads removed and treated separately elsewhere, presumably outside the manor house.

To examine fragmented head debris more accurately, an improved locational study was made of whole mandibles and loose deciduous fourth premolars of younger animals and late erupting third molars of older individuals (Wilson 1989a, Table 11). It established that the majority of sheep and cattle mandibles lay outside the manor buildings and that primary and/or secondary butchery of the carcasses of these species discarded most of the bones of heads and feet outside before the cooking of the disjointed and,or deboned portions of the carcasses of these two species. This argument should not be construed to mean that organs like the brain and tongue of sheep were not eaten. Probably they were consumed but they would have been removed from the heads before cooking and the cranial elements discarded outside.

For pigs the elemental bias differed markedly from sheep in

the exceptional proportion of metapodial bones present in Rooms A9 and A10. Head debris appeared more common than that of sheep. The more selective study of mandibles and teeth indicated that half the pig head debris lay inside the building and that differences in the species pattern were statistically significant.

Anomalies in the spread of pig bones made sense. Pig trotters, 'boars heads' and necks offered more edible tissues than the equivalent parts of sheep and have been highly regarded as delicacies. It was concluded that often these parts of pig were retained whole for cooking or pickling after butchery had taken place and possibly were discarded at a later stage than other carcass parts. Element percentages of pig bones may have been affected also by the preparation of bacon and ham but this factor only emphasised the importance of butchery as a distributive factor in the patterning of bones.

In Room A9 the representation of carcass parts of rabbit and hare resembled those of sheep. Only the elements of the main carcass as far as the neck, tibia and radius were present while a few cranial and foot bones were relatively more abundant farther away. Similarly for domestic fowl; elements of the head and feet were less common in internal building contexts than in external ones. This indicated that the heads and feet of these small animals were cut off during butchery and discarded away from the central concentration of most fine debris.

With fish the elements of the head, backbone and fins were abundant in the floor deposits and indicated that these skeletal parts were not commonly discarded when fish were cut up during salting, drying or cooking of whole or part fish, particularly the sea fishes.

All of this discussion implied that the small and fine debris inside the central and domestic rooms was primarily the remains of meals eaten at the table, that is of meat joints of medium sized carcasses and of carcasses of smaller mammals and birds cooked relatively entire but frequently without their heads and feet. Fish were cooked whole or in untrimmed fillets. Here was the fulfillment of previous theory, that the major bones of rabbit, hare, fowl and fish, and the bones in mutton and pork joints were most unlikely to have been boned out before cooking – except where meat was cured. Mere unranked room by room comparisons might not have detected these basically central to peripheral trends of bones and activities.

–0–

Besides the probable exclusion of whole heads and feet of sheep and rabbits, and some parts of pig, from cooking, the large size of beef carcasses would have predisposed the butchery of the cattle toward a separation of meat from the bones before cooking. The relative paucity of cattle bones amongst the debris which was argued to have been cooked therefore made sense from the viewpoints both of previous efficient butchery, the cooking of smaller pieces of beef, and the pre-empting of any need to clear beef bones with the rest

of the uneaten table waste.

It was possible though that beef bones were cooked sometimes as soups, stews or marrow for the table. If so theory and evidence indicated that most such bones would have been removed by rubbish clearance.

Beef bones may well have been chopped up and boiled for fat and glue – the former for tallow candles and soap. Almost invariably, the long bones in the collection were broken despite good preservation in other respects. They were more consistently smashed up than bones in Iron Age and some Romano–British collections. So table and other domestic use of marrow and other fatty tissues at the manor is almost certain.

Again, however, such bony remains appeared unlikely to be mixed with table refuse inside buildings although mixing of rubbish from different sources must have occurred outside the buildings. Fine debris was probably excluded from fat extraction as it would have been preferable to boil up the large bones rather than smaller ones which had been cooked once already.

Boiling up of bones might have taken place inside but bad odours might have relegated the fire place to the periphery of the domestic area. Greasy bone refuse was probably dumped outside.

–0–

It has been concluded that the rooms of Block A were domestic in function and were not farmyard buildings. Room A9, the purest repository of the surviving table refuse, lay between the service end of the main hall A1, and Rooms A12 and W which were interpreted by the excavator as the kitchens. A9 and A10, on either side of a connecting passage between hall and kitchens, were interpreted as the buttery and the pantry which, of course, refer to the storage of foodstuffs and kitchen and mealtable utensils. Storage purposes of these rooms cannot be confirmed because the bones there were probably table refuse although items like cold or preserved meats, for example the pig trotters, might have been kept there.

Meal tables of trestle type probably were put up in the main hall and other tables in A9 and A10 and the kitchen. Table wastes may have accumulated temporarily in A9 while meals were in progress and when refuse was cleared from the main hall tables. Much table waste could have been fed to pigs and poultry, dumped into pens or other places outside, such as in the courtyard where a concentration was noted; put into a midden for haulage as manure to the fields; or simply thrown outside the area of excavation, for example into the moat. Incomplete or careless clearance from tables and floors led to the gradual accumulation of bones in the floors.

Perhaps floors were kept cleaner by covering them with fresh earth and tamping it down. On the whole, despite hundreds of medium sized bones being found in some room floors, the number of bones exposed at any one time may have been small. Thus living conditions may not have been as squalid as the results at first may suggest for the domestic Rooms A9, A10 and A12.

The lower density of bones in the hall suggested that it was largely kept clean of refuse despite the high probability that much waste was created there at mealtables and especially during banquets. Room A3, the parlour, and nearby Rooms A4, A13 and A14 appeared to have been kept quite clean, parts of the building which are believed to have had higher household status.

Room A5, thought to have been the garderobe, apeared less well kept although much of the coarser disarticulated debris, a few skulls of cattle and pig, and a goose skeleton, probably were deposited during the abandonment of the house.

Rooms A12 and W seem to have been the kitchens where small carcases might have been butchered relatively whole and, with meat joints of larger animals, cooked carried out and served in the main hall. More elaborate preparation of food for feasts would have varied the economical and theoretical pattern of butchery proposed. Rabbit heads and paws, chicken feet and other ends may have been thrown outside, to dogs, cats and other animals, or were appropriated by the servants for their own food. Little of this type of butchery waste survived anywhere and least in the kitchen floors.

–0–

Slaughtering and the initial stages of butchery of animals, such as gutting, probably took place outside the kitchen, in another building or in the courtyard or farmyard, especially when it was necessary to deal with large carcases and avoid unnecessary mess, discomfort and hindrance of other kitchen activities. All the same, it is not that unusual to envisage the skinning and plucking of the smallest animals in the kitchen.

A sparse scatter of sheep head and foot debris occurred in the vicinity of Building H and indicated a possible slaughtering place of larger animals or where preliminary butchery waste was rendered by further industry. In a spatially well–differentiated household and farmyard like that of the manor, butchery of large and medium sized animals might have occurred in the same place, for example where equipment may have stood to hang carcasses.

Probable butchery waste of cattle and pig, although relatively abundant in nondomestic contexts, appeared meagre around farmyard Building foundations J to O and did not strengthen any argument on butchery location as based on the sheep bones. As some of the foundation structures included animal pens and Building H may have been a cattle byre, slaughtering there appeared inappropriate and butchery of cattle might have taken place closer to the domestic range of buildings than Buildings G, H, K and M. Encouragement to do so would have been given by the lesser distance to carry carcass halves, quarters or other joints and meaty organs.

Dumped earth or rubbish layers of F573 near Building E and domestic Block A contained a higher percentage of head and foot elements of cattle, although they lay adjacent to Rooms A1 and A3 which were believed to have had higher status. However areas of high status and cleanliness were probably limited by other functional considerations and probably confined to building interiors, such as of the chapel (Room A11) and possibly to any ornamental gardens.

In summary, theory and scanty bone evidence indicate that butchery of larger animals took place in one or two areas in the arc of Buildings E, A4, A5, F, W, B, J and I but perhaps within 10 m – 20 m of the domestic quarter, especially the kitchens.

Apart from the supposed byre, structural evidence of animal management on site gave few spatial clues to where animals were kept in the farmyard. Locations of part skeletons of two cats may indicate their association with the domestic quarter and its activities. Bones of a puppy were found in Building M and indicated a kennel nearby.

–0–

There are wider ramifications to site activities like those explored above. Besides domestic and farmyard matters, the farmstead should be seen as the nucleus of an arable and animal husbandry farm. Human organisation of manors was complicated and included interaction with the village in the desmene and with neighbouring manors like that at nearby Cuxham (Harvey 1965). Manors were part of a widespread rural and urban commercial network in which market centres evolved, and, at the highest level manors were part of and subject to a political and religious hierarchy. These relationships varied the pattern of food production and consumption at the manor.

Not all food was home produced. Seafish, shellfish like oysters, mussels and whelks, and crab were imported to Hardings Field, probably via London markets. Even some red meat came from elsewhere, such as venison from fallow deer. Woodland or parkland was probably absent from the land immediately around the manor house and implies the deer were killed and probably butchered some distance away. Perhaps other meat was brought in as exchanged products, gifts and obligations of medieval culture.

Comparable organizational complexity, albeit different in form, needs to be allowed, if only in our imagination, for cultures that are truly prehistoric like the one at Mingies Ditch.

–0–

Findings at the manor (Wilson 1989a and Wilson unpub. b) have few peers in the published literature for the interest of the well–preserved bones, their spatial context and for the clarification that site data give to the interpretation of archaeological sites. Coupled with Mingies Ditch report (Allen & Robinson 1993) these are the two most meaningful excavations in the region and possibly nationally in terms of current intrasite spatial analysis. With the writing of their reports the power of unifying and differentiating principles shone out from these derelict settlements of different existential complexity and cultural context and separated by over a thousand years of human endeavour.

Nontheless, looking back on these investigations, it is felicitous that the difficulties of sorting out and explaining the degraded bones at Mingies Ditch preceded work on the medieval material. To assert the authenticity of the Iron Age trends alone now seems a reckless reliance on one's intellect. None the less the teasing out of the elusive prehistoric spatial patterns has promoted a superior use of the higher quality medieval data in testing scientific ideas.

The implication that sites of different period and culture can be interpreted, to some extent, by general principles of human organisation may not appear radical within the developmental context of this book. Yet, viewed both by the kind of criteria which define the different past cultures of Britain and by the way in which site bone reports are usually presented (i.e. by cultural and chronological period), the sites of Mingies Ditch, Barton Court Farm and Hardings Field appear superficially as different in cultural character as one could expect of any three 'farmsteads' in a given region. Zoologically and spatially viewed, however, they appear much more closely related and more similar than 'culture orientated' archaeologists have implied until now. Yet these cross cultural and cross time similarities in spatial configurations of bones should be no surprise when emphasis has been given to the conservativeness which is inherent in such essential behaviour as the preparation, cooking and eating of meat and the use and disposal of other carcass parts.

It follows from the above that when one sets aside data which appears largely determined culturally, the main requirement for understanding basic human behaviour at settlements from species lists and bone frequencies is that the representation of individual species is less important than first obtaining general statements about the spatial pattern of different sized bone debris on the site.

Chapter 9

Regularities in Site Activities at Watkins Farm

Ahead of describing more complicated sites to follow, similarities of bone evidence to that already introduced occurred at a further excavation. Watkins Farm at Northmoor, Oxfordshire, was another low-lying site on the Thames gravels. Excavations took place during 1983 and 1985, directed by Tim Allen, and uncovered a ditched enclosure around the shallow somewhat complex remains of a number of scattered Middle Iron Age house gullies and other features with overlying linear or rectangular ditches of Roman date, Fig. 19. Many features had been damaged by topsoil stripping of gravel extractors but there remained enough information to obtain a general idea of the occupation of this damp, predominently pastoralist settlement.

Findings and discussion of the site have been published (Allen 1990). In investigating the bones according to previous spatial and ecocultural considerations, results were presented in the report first, particularly by Table 17 (Wilson 1990a, Table T9). This ranks feature groups of bones in terms of the percentages of sheep and pig bones and of burnt and worked debris as indices of former domestic activity. Higher percentages coincided with the location of definitely identified houses, e.g. the central roundhouse, and usefully indicated the presence of other houses or hearths where features scarcely survived. Other indications of domestic activity later confirmed my conclusions (Allen 1990, Table 14).

At this site it was not possible to show confidently the outward spread of coarse debris although the evidence was not inconsistent with what would be expected. This is because the main Iron Age enclosure ditch (MED) was largely redug in the early Roman period, obliterating the dating evidence in the earlier trench, and perhaps may not legitimately be compared with the house site debris. Even though the ditch contained coarse debris which would normally confirm the theory of spatial analysis, it is possible that the bones reflect an intensifying reliance over time in cattle and horse husbandry at the settlement, culture which appears characteristic of the Romano-British occupation.

In terms of making further interpretations according to theory, it was noted that the debris from the central roundhouse, particularly in phase 3 the most abundant bone group, and other houses appeared to have a higher concentration of coarse debris present, including a higher representation of horse. This may be explained by the somewhat greater distances between the Iron Age houses than at Mingies Ditch. The outward location and radiation of coarse debris by scavenging, rubbish clearance and butchery place, was more likely to accumulate in the gullies of relatively distant houses than in features of houses closer together as at Mingies Ditch. Thus, in addition to its own medium sized debris, the central roundhouse received coarse debris from houses surrounding it. This logic suggests that

Table 17 **Primary assessment of all the depositional contexts of bone groups at Watkins Farm in terms of their probable proximity to former centres of domestic activity**

	Number of bones	Combined % of sheep and pig (high % to indicate greater dom. activity)	% of burnt and worked bones	Vector assessment of domestic activity in rank order (highest = 1)
Iron Age groups				
a) Inside main enclosure				
S house 23-32	197	59	5.1	1
Central roundhouse				
phases 1 and 2	163	52	4.3	3
phase 3 + trackway	364	40	2.8	4
phases 3/4 and 5	136	46	2.2	5
E house 124-163	100	42	1.0	7
W house 496, 513 etc.	108	33	5.5	2
W enclosure 436-442	41	32	2.2	6
b) Enclosures outside MED				
NW 485, 490 etc.	16	50	-	8
SW 17-20 etc.	26	23	-	14
Early Romano-British gps.				
Main encl. ditch MED	111	12	-	15
Ditches inside MED 405etc.	158	21	1.9	12
Int. features on E 96 etc.	123	36	-	13
Ext. E encl. 12-13 etc.	86	15	2.4	11
Ext. W encls. 24,28 etc.	45	36	-	13
Later R-B groups				
All encls. & trkwy ditches	179	34	1.1	9
Waterholes/pits 412 etc.	36	3	-	16
Site B				
All R-B features	206	14	4.8	10

Note: Groups within Romano-British periods could be reranked from 1 especially since such groups contain higher percentages of cattle bones due to cultural factors
From Wilson 1990a.

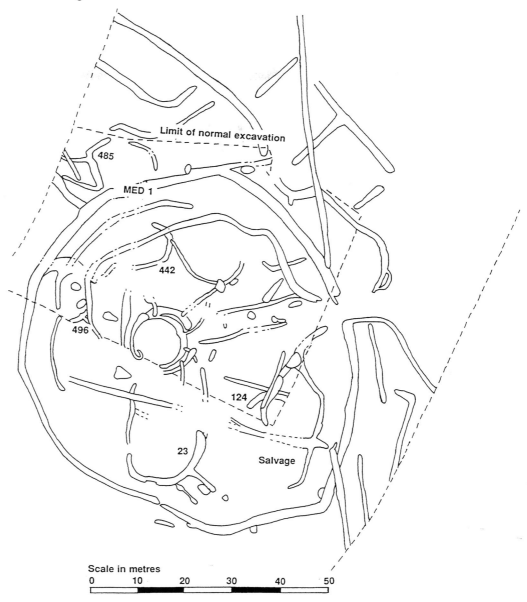

Fig. 19. Simplified plan of the main enclosure system and house enclosures at Watkins Farm (after Allen 1990).

the coexistence of other houses (and their domestic activity and the spreading of their coarse bones) on site occurred most at middle (phase 3) and later phases of the long occupied central roundhouse.

Another minor factor acting on the bone distribution was evidence that the bones of horse and cattle were utilised in the working of bone by craftsmen. Thus some bones of the large species would be kept or discarded close to hearths and houses as raw and waste material of craft activity.

Bone evidence from a comparison of feature type groups with other Iron Age sites (Wilson 1990a, Fig. A4) shows generally that features at Watkins Farm contained relatively more coarse debris than some feature type groups elsewhere. One may be able to go on and conclude this could be related also to cultural factors of specialising in Iron Age cattle and horse rearing and to dampland conditions encouraging stock rearing of the two species at the expense of sheep, as suggested for the small Farmoor house enclosures (Wilson

1978b, 135–6). Alternatively, it may be related to the observation that occupation layers, like those at Mingies Ditch, appear to contain many sheep and pig bones, but sooner or later were destroyed at most sites including Watkins Farm, thus obscuring the true contribution of these species in the site results.

In looking at the results the impression is given that house gullies at several sites contain coarser material than might be expected given their proximity to the buildings. This would indicate that domestic or table refuse and fireash was not thrown directly into house gullies but rather onto ground surfaces around houses. Ash, bone debris and gravel dug from features would serve some use in solidifying ground around houses that might otherwise quickly turn to mud with trampling from people and stock. Larger fragments, however, would still have been scattered from the ground surfaces and accumulated in deeper features nearby as well as further afield.

PART III

COMPLEX LANDSCAPES AND LARGE SETTLEMENTS

Differentiation...... describes the ways through which the main social functions or the major institutional spheres of society become disassociated from one another, attached to specialised collectivity and roles, and organized in relatively specific and autonomous symbolic and organizational frameworks within the confines of the same institutionalized system (Eisenstadt 1967, 215).

......it must be stressed just how different a town is, as an archaeological site, from a rural site. ...... From this one fact spring most of the problems and constraints on the possible sampling strategies. Whereas in rural sampling the sites chosen are usually open to any excavation strategy, including 'total' excavation, in the town the archaeologist has no choice but to sample......(Wade 1978, 279).

Chapter 10

Widespread Iron Age and Romano–British Occupation Layers at Claydon Pike, Gloucestershire

Until this stage of the text the most important analyses gone into have been of relatively simple rural settlements and at best of a single cultural period. Around 1979 the regional excavation strategies of the Oxford Unit became more ambitious and developed with the concept of investigating extensive areas of ancient landscapes rather than focussing on the excavation of single small settlements. Not only were settlements part of a wider landscape, they and the landscape were seen to be differentiated into a complex overall entity – a probable influence of the earlier method of site catchment analysis. While noticeable differentiation of human activities in the landscape goes back to the Neolithic period, the growth of towns and cities is very much evident in the archaeological record from the Iron Age to the Roman period and from the late Saxon to modern periods.

The best example of early settlement differentiation investigated in the Upper Thames Valley is illustrated by the extensive excavations at Claydon Pike, near Fairford, on the border between Oxfordshire and Gloucestershire. Digging was directed by David Miles and Simon Palmer between 1980 and 1984 (Miles & Palmer 1981, 1982 and 1983). A Middle Iron Age settlement, of clustering houses and enclosures (dug previously), appeared succeeded by a Late Iron Age settlement some distance away and which, in turn, became differentiated into a Roman settlement of four distinct parts and covering an area of around 180 m x 100 m, the largest total excavation undertaken by the Oxford Unit.

Despite lengthy deliberation over results, little concrete can be concluded about the spatial organisation of the Middle Iron Age settlement. Subsequent settlement remains are more interesting. A plan of the Late Iron Age and Romano–British settlement features at Claydon Pike is provided to show major site structures and the platforms of gravel they stood on, Fig. 20. On Platform I a mass of features was cut into the gravel including circular Late Iron Age enclosures, successive large multiroomed Romano–British farmhouses (labelled B1, B2, B7, B8 and B9) surrounded by subrectangular ditches and superficial remains of a large building (B3) to the east. Situated on Platform II were rectangular enclosures and features of insubstantial Romano–British buildings, including one labelled B4, perhaps cottages. Platform III embodied further rectangular and other features of scarcely surviving structures while Platform IV had rectangular enclosures and traces interpreted as a temple or temenos. Linking the four platforms with features were ditches thought to define trackways.

Whether the Romano–British settlement should be called a villa complex, village or imperial farm is debateable. Regardless, the spread of bone debris at the site presages the complexity of patterning such as the division of labour expected to be found in larger and more populous communities of people living together.

At this site the deeper features indicated the structures which stood there but the most informative bone debris occurred in the occupation layers lying above the gravel–cutting features and under the topsoil. These layers survived because this ground had only recently been converted from permanent pasture to arable ploughland. Uppermost levels contaminated with non Roman pottery were not included in the detailed analysis of bones.

In 1985 I began recording the bones from the settlement and grouped the bone data from the layers within the 10 m x 10 m squares or quadrats of the site grid which was the smallest mapping unit common to all the data groups and gave greater reliability to sample numbers in outermost areas where bones were spread thinly.

Large numbers of bones were found in sample areas across the site, most occurring in the area of Platform I and particularly above and in association with the Romano–British farmhouse(s), rather than with the Iron Age features and suggesting residual Iron Age debris was insufficient to distort the interpretation of later bone patterns. Some allowance for the complexity of phasing over four centuries is needed although this need not be specified here.

The examination of Fig. 21 began what came to be referred to as 'primary analysis,' (see Table 17) or the preliminary assessment of taphonomic processes of bone deposition on sites. Percentages of sheep and pig bones on this map showed concentrations of this type of bone debris at the approximate centres of all four areas of the site. According to previous work this indicated domestic activities in these places, even where structural remains scarcely survived.

A comparable plot of the percentage index of domestic fowl and goose bones confirmed the presence of domestic activity on Platforms I and II. To some extent, however, the distribution of these bird bones appeared dependent on the evidence of Fig. 22 which is a map of the amount of bone degradation of bone groups in quadrats by using the percentage index of sheep bones employed in the analysis of bones at Mingies Ditch.

At Claydon Pike the most degraded bone groups occurred around the periphery of Platforms I and II and extensively over Platform III. The pattern was partly explained by some of the upper level occupation layer over Platform I containing modern ceramic sherds ploughed into it and the bone data from it being excluded from the primary analysis. Thus only data from the deeper and better preserved bones from Platform I remained for consideration.

The distribution of bird bones therefore appeared to be according to their survival in thicker deposits. The same reasoning might therefore explain the higher percentages of sheep and pig bones at the centres of the four platform areas. However, this appeared not to be a major factor since the

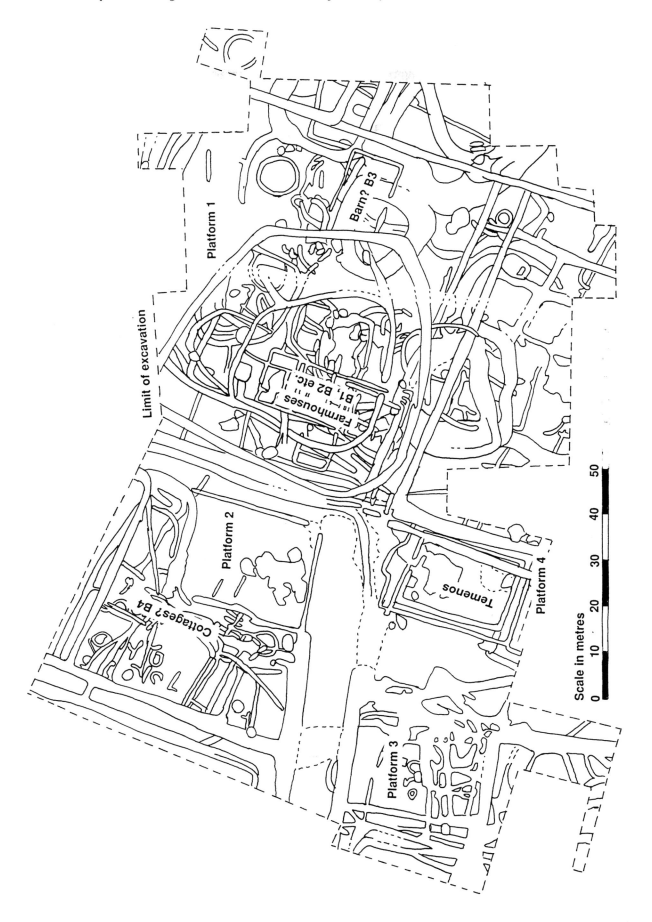

Fig. 20. Plan of Iron Age and Romano–British features at Claydon Pike (after Hingley and Miles 1984).

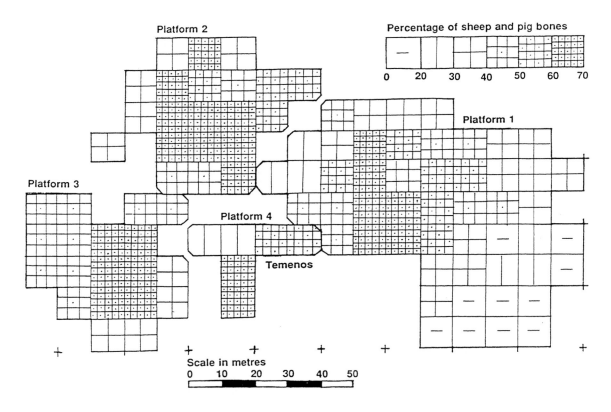

Fig. 21. Percentages of medium sized debris (sheep and pig bones) in the grid squares of occupation layers at Claydon Pike.

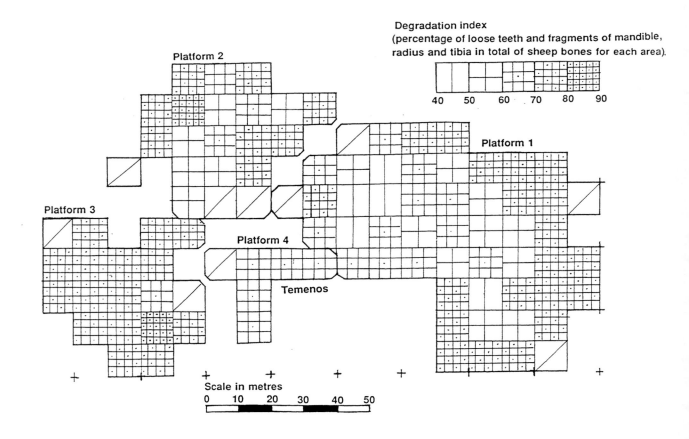

Fig. 22. Distribution of percentages of bones based on the degradation of sheep bones in the grid squares at Claydon Pike.

54

central to peripheral distribution of degraded bones (measured by the degradation index) was opposite that at Mingies Ditch where the most degraded bones occurred in the central areas of domestic activity as indicated by medium coarse debris. Since the species pattern of medium coarse bones there had survived severe bone degradation, it was unlikely that much species pattern yielding debris on the periphery of the platforms at Claydon had disappeared due to bone degradation.

It was therefore concluded that the bone distributions of sheep and pig at both sites were authentic patterns and that the more complex spread of coarse and medium sized debris at Claydon Pike displayed essentially the same central to peripheral trends as other sites examined previously. Here the centres of each of the four site areas had its own focus of domestic activity.

On Platform I the concentration of sheep, pig and bird bones confirmed the interpretation of the large multiroomed buildings as successive farmhouses and centres of domestic activity. Unfortunately the bones in this area did not reveal the locations of any specialised rooms like kitchens although a few worked bones in the vicinity of Buildings B2, B7 and B9 indicated some specialised craft activities occurred in that area. Results of other artefact studies by Robert Rippengal may help here.

East of the farmhouses, the other large building, Building B3, did not stand in an island of concentrated sheep and pig bones and almost certainly was a non domestic and farmyard building. This deduction helps to confirm the prior interpretation of this building as a barn. Some worked bones lay to the south and were indicative of other specialised activities nearby or the dumping of their remains from elsewhere.

On Platform II the accumulation of pig and sheep bones there indicated that Building B4 and others may have been largely domestic in function and, since the building foundations were not substantial, perhaps had lower status occupants than at the farmhouse(s) on Platform I.

The spread of burnt bones was more complicated and difficult to interpret; it partly overlapped higher concentrations of domestic debris about buildings and extended outside them, Fig. 23. On the first three platforms the spreads of burnt bones might have indicated the removal of burnt refuse from hearths to the outside of buildings or it reflected bones burnt incidentally by the fires of outdoor activities like the burning of rubbish.

On the fourth platform there were much higher percentages of burnt bones, particularly on the north side of the temple near its probable entrance from the settlement. This indicates hearths connected with the ritual functioning of the temple. A high proportion of burnt debris and the small numbers of bones overall within the ritual area might indicate clearance of burnt debris from the temple to the exterior and the entrance. Alternatively, the bones were burnt by fire(s) at the temple entranceway. A scatter of sheep and pig bones within

suggested 'domestic activity' there but could have accumulated within a ritual context, rather like the dense accumulation of bones at the ritual complex of Uley Hill (Ellison 1981) although the identification of abundant goat bones there is a much stronger indicator of ritual activity than can be concluded for the rectangular enclosure at Claydon Pike.

Unfortunately the study of other bones from deeper, more discrete features added little to the pattern and interpretation of the spatial patterns of bones given above. One exception to this was the record of butchery marks and their interpretation which has been briefly outlined in the discussion of Iron Age and Romano-British butchery in chapter 6.

About this stage of investigating sites and writing bone reports, my health broke down in 1985 and effectively ended my fulltime contribution to the programme of work of the Oxford Unit. Ultimately the report on the bones from Claydon Pike was written, based on my data, information and resume, by Bruce Levitan, my successor (Wilson & Levitan unpub.).

A paper on the findings of the spatial analyses at all sites was intended to be given to the annual conference of the Association for Environmental Archaeology which was being held in Groningen, The Netherlands, that year. The conference theme was 'Manmade Soils' which seemed appropriate. However, hospitalisation meant I could not attend the conference. The will to complete the work faded and the manuscripts were put aside. Months later I began to take an interest in academic affairs again.

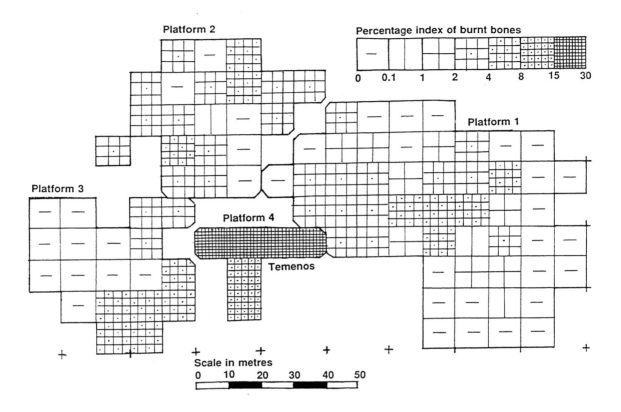

Fig. 23. Distribution of the percentage index of burnt bones in the grid squares at Claydon Pike.

Chapter 11

Spatial Diversification of Activities in Towns: Late Saxon to Post–Medieval Oxford and Abingdon

The last chapter of my first draft manuscript on 'Spatial patterns of bones in archaeological deposits' was to examine the literature and findings from the largest settlements in the region with the aim of describing the spatial organisation of bone–related town life. Unlike the forward planning of discovering spatial distributions of bones at rural sites, however, town sites had been investigated primarily with the aim of determining their Saxon, Roman and Iron Age origins and not in coherent spatial sampling and digging programmes that allowed for the complexity of town deposition.

Unlike most rural sites, urban ones of much duration built up a deep accumulation of soil and bones, sometimes several metres deep as in Abingdon (Wilson, Thomas & Wheeler 1979) and much deeper in parts of Oxford. Deep excavations, of course, are difficult to implement and the revealed stratigraphy is likely to be limited and complicated, such as with the redeposition of older material in later features. More importantly the horizontal placement and relationship of building structures and bone layers is rarely able to be investigated to any extent because excavations investigating the development of living towns are typically much more restricted by available space, time and money than excavations of rural sites. At least that has been the Oxford digging experience.

On the other hand it is possible to treat the smaller and spatially limited trenches in each town as sample holes of a broadscale and long term plan of investigating the whole settlement and its activities in space and historical sequence.

–0–

There are further difficulties in the exploration of large settlements. The first towns might be traced as far back as the hillforts or oppida of the Iron Age but those in the region are poorly investigated.

When the Roman period is surveyed, the towns and military forts in the region were few, sparsely spread and not well investigated or published in terms of their bones. Excavators have dug into the major Roman towns of Cirencester and Silchester and into minor centres of Abingdon, Alchester, Dorchester–on–Thames and Towcester but only one contrast of reported bones along the lines of my spatial investigation is yet evident. At Towcester, Northamptonshire, one collection of bones from Park Street contained 54% of sheep and pig bones (Payne 1980) while a very small group from elsewhere in the town contained predominantly cattle and horse bones (Jones unpub.).

One possible problem of interpreting such bone data of this period is that increased percentages of cattle and pig bones are held to indicate the extent that settlements were Romanised and thus less Celtic in their culture (King 1978).

Also percentages of horse bones appear greater at rural sites

(Wilson 1986 and unpub. c) than in town sites like Dorchester–on–Thames (Grant 1978 and 1980). Careful intrasite comparisons of more extensively dug towns, however, should overcome these interpretive difficulties.

While the determination of the organisation of Roman towns elsewhere has made progress, for example at Exeter (Maltby 1979), that around the Upper Thames region must largely be left to future investigations. Rather more can be said about late Saxon and medieval Oxford.

–0–

Much of interest in the archaeology of Oxford has already been popularized and brought up to date (Hassall 1987). Although bones, environment, animal life and domestic activity around the town and city has not received great public attention, this can be rectified here and elsewhere (Harman 1985; Robinson & Wilson 1987, 65–70; Wilson 1980b; 1984a; 1989b and unpub. d and e).

A guide to city excavation sites mentioned in the text is given in Fig. 24. While many of the excavations have yielded only small glimpses of past urban activities, it is worth applying the ideas learnt from rural spatial studies to current bone information and trying to make sense of the settlement distribution of bone debris as a whole (Wilson unpub. f).

Consequently, our main marker of domestic activity, the percentage of medium sized debris (i.e. of sheep and pig bones in the total of the bones of the four commonest species) was calculated for 21 early Oxford sites. Figures were given for 10th– to 13th– century groups, with one exception of longer duration. Most of these percentages have been plotted at site locations on an outline map of Saxon and medieval Oxford, Fig. 25. Contour lines at 10% intervals were sketched by inspection among the find spot results to indicate the greatest concentrations of sheep and pig bones, i.e. medium coarse debris, in the town at the period under scrutiny. Highest percentages indicate the main areas occupied by Saxon and Norman households and rubbish dumps.

Although one assumption is that the domestic waste of Oxford was not carried very far to dump, in principle any deviation from this assumption should not be too much of a problem since, by our explanatory model, coarser refuse from butchery of large carcasses was also liable to end up in the more distant deposits; it would dilute any pure household waste and should therefore be detectable by post–excavation analysis.

In looking at the mapping of domestic activity, one becomes aware of difficulties like sampling bias and other errors of method. One feels that more sample places would yield a more complicated urban pattern and averaging and weighting of results could be necessary to even out variable results due

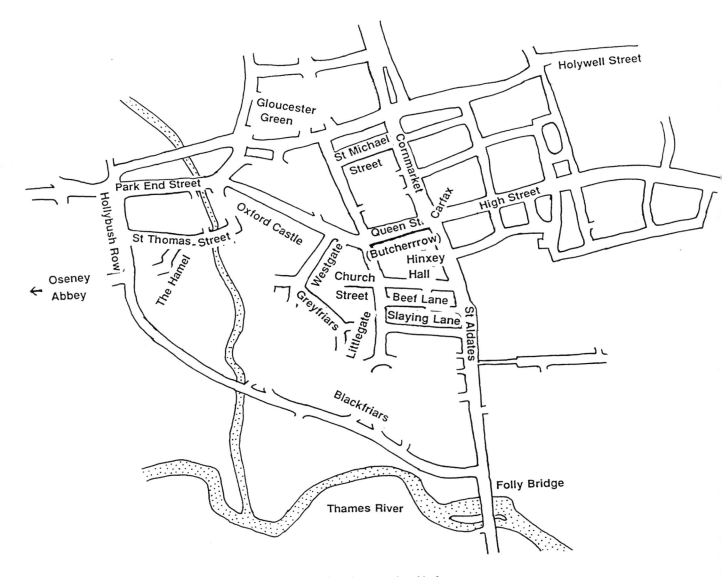

Fig. 24. Map of Oxford places mentioned in the text.

to small sample sizes and unreliable figures from the earliest excavations where bone recovery may not have been a dig priority.

Adventurous method or not, the results obtained appear to be the first time a town has been mapped by its domestic bone refuse; material which was spread over an area of perhaps 1 km by 0.6 km and therefore is some measure of a settlement which was some twentyfive times larger than the already sizeable excavation of the Claydon Pike Roman settlement. Actually, the sparse coarser town refuse is estimated, by reference to the previous settlement refuse modelling and observation of bone spreads, to cover a much greater area than indicated on the map.

Thus the mapping exercise and a somewhat arbitrary 60% contour may broadly define the extent of 10th- to 12th-century Oxford houses. Exclusively 12th- and 13th- century deposits from Littlegate, The Hamel, and Blackfriars were allowed for although not plotted on the map as they were

somewhat later extensions west and south in the suburban growth of the town. Information for the later medieval period is limited and a similar map of it would be quite distorted by sampling difficulties in comparison to the one drawn.

Skeptics might claim that the map portrays nothing new about Saxon Oxford but some observations of it are worth making. Topographically, domestic refuse and, thereby, domestic activity is most in evidence for the brow (along High and Queen Streets) and the south facing slope from the second river gravel terrace down to the first one and as far as Folly Bridge. Many houses may well have been built in this zone although Hinxey Hall is the only one excavated (Halpin 1983). In the west, Saxon domestic activity on the interterrace slope preceded the Norman construction of the castle which altered town layout considerably and affected later deposition.

Far less domestic activity is evident for the flat northern part

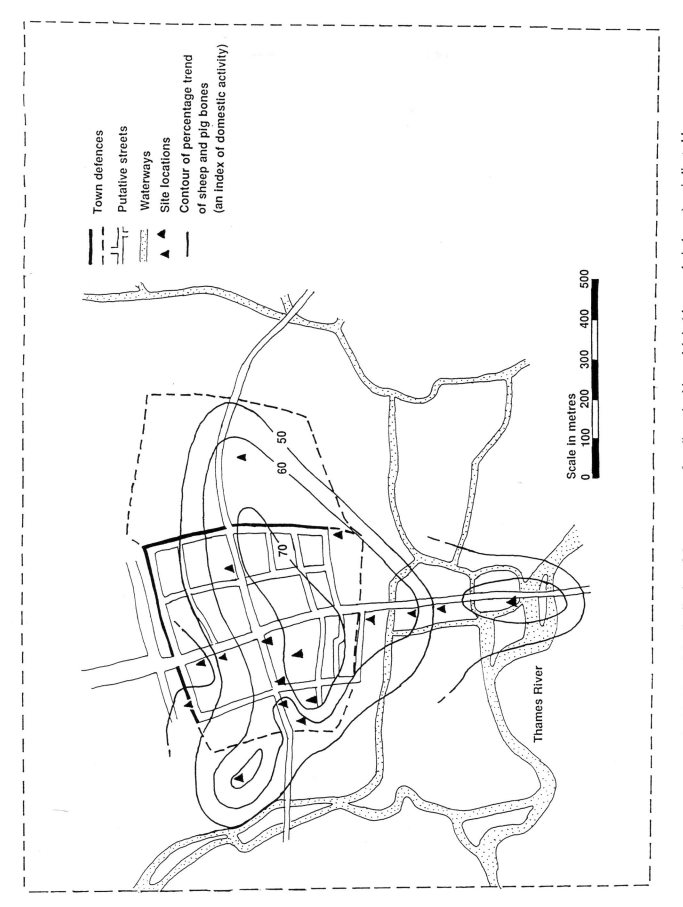

Town defences

Putative streets

Waterways

Site locations

Contour of percentage trend of sheep and pig bones (an index of domestic activity)

50

60

70

Thames River

Scale in metres

0 100 200 300 400 500

Fig. 25. Map of the distribution of the percentage of medium sized bone debris (sheep and pig bones) as indicated by contour lines around site samples from late Saxon and early medieval Oxford.

of the second terrace and the town north of the High Street, including land behind the northern Saxon defences. This last observation may only stem from a deficiency of reliable bone recovering excavations in the north and east quarters of Oxford. Alternatively, results might indicate more open and less occupied ground there with other nondomestic types of activity, perhaps gardening or the coralling of livestock, especially in times of siege (Wilson unpub. e). The few indications of settlement to the north and east may help explain why colleges of the university were mainly built in these parts of town.

During the late- and post- medieval periods there is evidence for a variety of microenvironments outside town buildings, such as areas of open pits, waste ground, gardens, orchards, pigsties and fowlyards. Besides pigs and chickens foraging whereever allowed, dogs and especially the scrawny cats would have been very much part of the scavenging of all manner of waste including bones as, probably, were wild animals such as foxes, hedgehogs, feral pigeons, crows, kites and ravens (Wilson 1984a and 1989b).

Household rubbish clearance activities are clearly evident in the large number of pits containing many animal bones, especially at Church Street, and dating often to the 12th and 13th centuries as well as to other periods. The prevalence of pits in medieval towns is in contrast to the manor site at Hardings Field where there were almost no pits at all. Although the town pits appear dug for gravel for roads and paths, they also served as convenient repositories for town rubbish, including cess. While medium coarse debris was abundant in excavated pits, it appears not quite as abundant and fine as in internal deposits like the floors at Hardings Field. Such debris was common in internal deposits at Hinxey Hall, Oxford, so that household debris in pits appears one or two steps coarser, presumably due to mixing with larger bone debris from other sources but nevertheless fairly directly dumped into pits and probably from houses nearby. The bones are just a minute part of the accumulation of household rubbish and construction and demolition debris that raised the level of streets and tenements over the centuries of urban activity.

–0–

Medieval and post–medieval urban butchery was quite distinct from the butchery of Iron Age and Roman rural sites as decribed previously in chapter 6. There are two main differences. First, as the medieval period advanced, more and more sheep and cattle carcasses appear halved down the backbone as indicated by the many split vertebrae. Carcasses were divided into halves and, probably, into quarters and other joints although the exact pattern is not known. This pattern almost certainly resulted from butchery of carcasses hung up by one method or another for meat cutting.

As the population of towns and cities grew, part–time butchers changed to full–time occupations and, with increasing demand for meat and a want to process carcasses efficiently, methods of butchery changed, at least with the largest businesses in the trade.

The second difference from early butchery practices was that there was an increasing trend to remove the heads and feet of sheep and cattle, probably at an early stage of butchery, and to treat them separately from the butchery of the main carcass. At least there are trends for the skeletal elements of the head and foot to be found separately from the elements of the main meat carcass.

This pattern is most clearly to be seen for sheep. Foot and hoof elements appear often removed with the skin. Sometimes during skin processing the feet and hooves were detached and thrown away directly (Wilson 1975). More commonly, these body parts were processed further, usually chopped up and boiled, probably for fat and protein which were made into tallow candles, soap and glue (Wilson 1989c and unpub. g and Wilson & Wallis 1991).

Sheep heads were probably removed after skinning. Splitting of the heads to remove the brains was quite a common, albeit age old, practice, sometimes the skulls being dumped separately by butchers (Wilson 1980b and 1989a and Wilson, Bramwell & Wheeler 1979) or sold with the brains to householders and being dumped with kitchen and table refuse. Sometimes the skulls had the horns lopped off them by the butcher (Wilson, Bramwell & Wheeler 1979).

Butchery of cattle heads and feet is less certainly known. Bones of the feet have been found in sufficient numbers to indicate their separate treatment, perhaps for fat extraction and neatsfoot oil (Sergeantson 1989) but often other cattle carcass elements are mixed up with foot elements to indicate common treatment by marrow extraction in domestic and trade processing. Sometimes the metapodial or cannon bones of cattle were collected in quantities and jammed together and upright to form floors of buildings located along Park End, Holywell and other streets in Oxford (Armitage 1989).

Cattle heads had the horns lopped off them, often being removed with the skins and only later being detached from them. The horny plating was removed by soaking and cutting and worked into useful or other saleable objects (MacGregor 1991, 355–78). Bony horn cores accumulated around tanneries but sometimes large numbers of cores were used as construction material, to line pits or ditches or build walls (Armitage 1984). Calf heads appear treated differently, the bones ending up amongst domestic refuse more commonly than bones from heads of adult cattle. Calf heads probably were sold at the butchers for brawn.

Bones of the main cattle carcass were probably separated from their surrounding meat at the butchers but seem to have travelled several pathways to their final resting places by domestic and trade processing, rubbish clearance and scavenging.

Earliest evidence of this differentiation of butchery refuse is indicated at Littlegate and Folly Bridge, Oxford, during the 12th and 13th centuries but such remains are more common during the late medieval period and standard practice from the 16th century onwards in Abingdon, Bicester, Buckingham and Oxford (Robinson & Wilson 1987, 71).

The placing and spacing of these activities in large settlements is mainly what interests us here. Theory of this is limited to a few general expectations about butchery and fellmongery activities. Division of labour and trade specialisation and differentiation of waste through space are expected as indicated above. Location of activities in relation to necessary resources, like water or fuel, would be other factors although site locations sometimes deny these expectations (Cherry 1991). Placing of butchery stalls and shops near marketing spaces appears an important consideration, bearing in mind the tendency to slaughter animals as close as convenient to domestic activity in small settlements.

Dwelling on the last requirement and considering that specialised trades and professions are a characteristic of large settlements, one or or two central places where butchery took place would seem to satisfy both domestic and trade wants. This seems to explain the presence of the first recorded meat market in the High Street of Oxford during the 12th and 13th centuries. Documentary mentions show that animals were slaughtered there and this is supported by a scatter of coarse debris found in the High Street kennel or mid street gutter. Cattle horn cores were the most prominent remains and indicate the storage of horns for working or storage of skins for leatherworking if not the skinning of carcasses nearby (Wilson unpub. g). Thus slaughtering, butchery, sale of meat and possibly the utilisation of other carcass products, all would seem to have taken place in close proximity to the High Street.

Into the 14th and 15th centuries, as animals were butchered close to the butchers stalls and the paths of meat buyers, the intensity of butchery and the inability or indifference of butchers to clear slaughtering wastes from the High Street resulted in complaints about the offensiveness of the area and its practices to shoppers. Consequently, the city burgesses forced the butchers by law to relocate their slaughtering and preliminary butchery away from their stalls and from households. This regulation pushed such business to the southern and possibly the western periphery of the city and, in particular, to streets which became known as 'Slaying Lane', now Brewer Street, and 'Beef Lane.' Thus an aesthetic component, concerning appearance, odour, notions and evaluations of pollution, etc, was important in determining trade activity locations.

This organisational and spatial change offered shorter distances to waste land and the Thames River where butchery refuse could be dumped with less offense to citizens of Oxford. Not surprisingly, the change is marked by alterations in the nature of site refuse in the town. From around the 14th century, head debris of adult cattle is less common and calf head debris more common in household refuse, because, as indicated above, most adult cattle head debris was dumped separately away from domestic refuse contexts, either direct from slaughterhouses or from semi

industrial sites processing carcass products like skins.

Other changes in the location of butchery stalls occurred. In 1556 most were moved perhaps 50 m from High Street to Queen Street, which was then named Butcher Row, presumably to allow greater room for other activities in the market around Carfax. Around 1773, perhaps to avoid growing congestion of street traffic, the stalls were relocated some 100 m away in the covered market just off the High Street. Evidence of the location of butchers stalls is minimal since most carcass waste would be discarded from the slaughterhouses or from domestic households or the colleges. Nonetheless small groups of 17th and 18th century sheep skulls were found during the digging at Westgate and Church Street and may have been butchers' waste from stalls in Butcher Row.

Outside the city walls at The Hamel, halved sheep skulls were abundant in a 16th century pit but probably resulted from the activities of a local butcher supplying meat in St Thomas's Parish market in its own High Street nearby.

Some sheep heads, however, reached households and clearly some split heads were for sale from butchers stalls. Even in these modern days of slickly packed, often boneless and somewhat bland supermarket meats, it has been possible occasionally to buy halved sheep and calf heads from the more traditional butchers in the covered market in Oxford.

From all of this evidence it is clear that the location of the essentially centralised selling place of meat is, and has been for centuries, considered the most important factor in the location of the different stages of butchery. As well as the moving of slaughterhouses to the periphery of Oxford, the tanneries also appear to have been located peripherally, at least from the late medieval period onwards.

A *c*17th– century tannery was located on the first river terrace 50 m from the Greyfriars and a c19th century one 100 m away. Many 18th– century cattle horn cores lining a pit at Greyfriars appear brought a short distance from one of the tanneries. Horn core groups of 13th century date also occurred at The Hamel and may indicate a tannery or hornworking there. Several tanners occupied buildings at the site and possibly at Hollybush Row where foot bones were made into floors. All these sites and also a tannery at Oseney Abbey nearby stood on lowlying land and were near a water supply from river channels. In other cities some former tanneries were not always located close to rivers (Cherry 1991) so may have obtained their water from wells.

Processing of foot debris of sheep and cattle is not much in evidence in Oxford although indicated by small peripherally located samples of bones at Littlegate, Folly Bridge, St Michael Street and Hollybush Row, again at the periphery of the 12th– and 13th– century town. Foot bones built into floors in different parts of the town could have been transported some distance from their processing source.

It would make sense if trades and industries using animal products were located close to slaughterhouses where raw

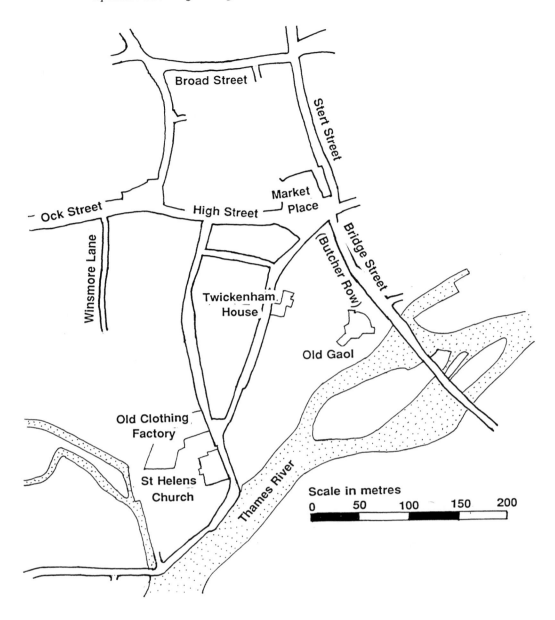

Fig. 26. Map of mentioned places in Abingdon and the peripheral location of sheep foot bone debris (see text).

materials were obtained. This appears to be the pattern in Oxford and also at St Peters Street, Northampton (Harman 1981), where both cattle horn cores and sheep foot bones were abundant among the remains of a late and post medieval tannery pit and building complex.

In this respect medieval and later excavations in Abingdon are of relevance. Best known location of slaughtering and butchery occurred at the Old Gaol site where there was a tenement owned in 1556 by a Widow Wyks, backing onto the Thames River and about 75 m from butchers stalls on Butcherrow, now Bridge street, Fig. 26. A 16th century pit of whole sheep foot bones on the site indicated direct dumping from the slaughterhouse or from skinworkers in the vicinity (Wilson 1975, 120). Some butchery refuse could have been thrown directly into the river as seems to have happened upriver in Oxford and downriver in London.

Sheep foot bones also occur farther along and downstream of

the Abingdon riverfront and in a farther arc around the periphery of the medieval town as far as Winsmore Lane (Wilson 1990b). Typically these foot bones were broken up by chopping and were almost certainly boiled up for tallow and glue. In one instance bones at Twickenham House were found close to a property owned by Thomas Knight and his son who were 18th and 19th century soap boilers, tallow chandlers and grocers (Wilson & Wallis 1991).

Much of the foot bone debris appeared part of dumping to raise the level of lowlying land and, near St Helens Church, on to land specifically called the 'town waste' in the 14th century and *'stinking ditches and filthy dunghills'* at a later date. This deposition took place from the late medieval period to the 19th century or later (Wilson 1989c). Occasional deposits of post-medieval cattle horn cores also occurred among the spread of the foot bones. All this refuse may well have originated at the Old Gaol site slaughterhouse and also from another post-medieval slaughterhouse and butcher shop in Stert Street (Wilson, Bramwell & Wheeler 1979).

Locations of pre–19th century tanneries in the town are not documented except in Ock Street but the existence of an earlier skinners guild is noted. Moreover, at the Old Gaol rectangular pits dating around the 18th century were found above the 16th century skinning refuse and appear to be tanning pits. Thus here again was a complex of closely related and spatially adjacent trade activities on the periphery of a town and close to a river. Similar tannery locations on streams or springs occurred in Wantage. In both towns tanneries were still conveniently close to butcher stalls.

Like changes in Oxford, significant activities in the Abingdon complex also appear to have begun in the 14th century. Unlike the 18th century date of change of market location in Oxford, they continued until the early 19th century when there appears a slow transition toward the establishment of proper butcher shops instead of market stalls in the street.

Today the succeeding butcher shops are struggling competitively with the highly organised and far–flung supermarket chains which have slaughterhouses many miles from their retail units. Also, modern mechanised transport has transformed the older spatial organisation, both where animals were walked or carted to the town where they were butchered and consumed, and where meat was carried a short distance home from the stall or shop to cook; suburban sprawl now dictates a different organisation of housekeeping and shopping. Additionally, busy road traffic and pedestrian malls rule the ground where the butchers shambles once stood. A solitary butcher's stall on the back of a truck survives in a weekly market at Gloucester Green, Oxford, to remind us of older ways of meat marketing.

Chapter 12

Modern Table Refuse and Butchery Practices

In thinking about archaeological remains like those of urban Oxford in the last chapter, one is often drawn to an active consideration of present affairs and processes. Anthropologists travel to other countries to discover relevant aspects of the cultures in order to describe and explain how we humans are constituted in many different ecological and social ways. Sometimes, however, the study of how British cultures are comprised can be just as valuable. Experimental archaeology at Butser Hill, Hampshire, where ideas about Iron Age life are tested, is a well known research venture. Everyday processes, nevertheless, can also be observed closely in one's own backyard or even in the kitchen!

When relating how such observations and conclusions to how the past occurred, one also finds excavations of medieval and post–medieval settlements particularly useful with historical evidence to guide one's interpretations and explanations. In the lack of documentary evidence, interpretations can be made reasonably justifiably in the assumption that what occurred in the recent past was similar to what happens now – until shown or detecting the errors of our methods and conclusions, of course. Chapters 15 and 16 look at examples of cultural activities less explicitly covered by my modelling.

Earlier arguments have demonstrated how Hardings Field manor site was one of the best of our regional excavations in stimulating thought about common and relatively conservative processes of butchery, rubbish clearance and scavenging in a spatial context. Medieval urban sites too, with their spatially differentiated bone distributions, throw much light on how butchery and related trades were carried out.

During the period at which the bone debris of the major medieval sites were under investigation and rationalisation, the idea of table refuse seemed worth examining more closely, for it appeared to be a useful concept introduced briefly in the passage of archaeologists like Hodder on their way to other theoretical and practical issues but never clarified or exemplified properly. Besides looking at medieval site debris, it was worth looking at a modern sample of table refuse and considering the processes which created it.

For almost two years during 1982 and 1983 I put aside the bony remains of dinners at home in my Abingdon flat instead of throwing the bones out with the rest of the domestic rubbish. The bones were cleaned and kept dry, so they would not decay and smell, and put aside until enough had been collected for a good sized sample to analyse.

Quite literally the bones were table refuse; all remains of cooked food put on the table for eating. None of the bones of bought meat joints or whole animals like fish, and no shells of shellfish, needed removal before cooking. Thus there was

almost no debris that could be termed 'kitchen refuse,' that is waste which resulted from preparation of food there. Some domestic fowl eggshells were the only exception. Although fastidious cooks may have chosen to remove bones from meat before cooking, e.g. by cutting off fish heads, all flesh was purchased in sizes convenient for cooking, e.g. as mutton chops. In other words there was an absence of any real need to remove bones to assist in cooking the meat (some meat was cut into smaller portions but this usually applied to meat like stewing steak which came without bones). For example, where fish were bought, fillets of larger fish and sometimes whole small fish were purchased.

From another point of view there was no need to butcher this food further when any bones were easier to isolate and avoid after cooking the meat. Overall the buying, preparation and cooking of food was made easy by the preparation of food at butchers, poulterers, fishmongers and supermarkets in Oxford and Abingdon.

Naturally, or should one say 'culturally', what I chose to buy was brought about by my own day to day preferences within the broad spectrum of British social values concerning the supply and demand of food, and the availability of money to buy food. Feeding a family might well result in a different pattern of buying food and therefore determine the nature of table and kitchen refuse but, by and large, it could be argued that my refuse would not be atypical of 20th century British table refuse.

Having collected it, no time was found to record and analyse its significance until 1986. The results and their archaeological implications were presented to a conference on bone and shell remains in Bordeaux, France (Wilson 1989a).

Fig. 27 shows a comparison of all the kinds of my table refuse according to the percentage cost of the meat and other animal protein and according to the percentage weight of the leftover bones and shells. Percentage cost of the meats is the best indication of the quantities by weight of each kind of meat eaten.

Since this book is mainly concerned with more conspicuous remains, Table 18 focuses on the numbers and percentages of mammal, bird and fish bones and marine mollusc shells in the collection. Around 1,100 bones accumulated after two years of meat eating. Some differences between tabulated results and the percentages of species bones by weight were noted, the chief observation showing that rabbit and fish bones were relatively more abundant than their bone weight indicated. Overall results showed that sheep, pig, rabbit and fish bones, or medium and small sized debris, were abundant in the table refuse. Fish bone weight did not indicate the sizeable contribution of fish to the diet. Cattle bones were not common at all and their weight was relatively

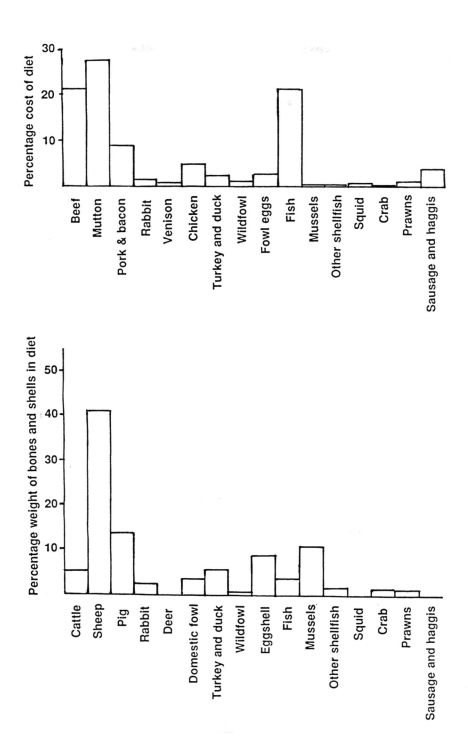

Fig. 27. Percentage cost and percentage by weight of the bones and shells of a modern meat diet (from Wilson 1989a).

Table 18 Fragment frequency, percentages of
mammal bones and percentage indicies
of other species bones and marine shells
in table refuse of a modern diet

	Frequency	%
Cattle	12	4.1
Sheep	155	52.9
Pig	61	20.8
Fallow deer	1	0.4
Total identified(n)	292	
Unidentified bones	271	

	Frequency	% index of n[3]
Fish vertebrae	410[2]	151.3
Chicken	31[2]	11.4
Duck	35[2]	12.9
Turkey	3	1.1
Pigeon	56[2]	20.7
Mussel	71	56.2
Scallop	1	0.4

[1] = Only vertebrae of fish were recorded
[2] = Results include articulated bones
[3] = Percentages of other species bones in
relation to the total number of identified mammal bones (n)
From Wilson 1989a.

Table 19 Percentages of grouped and single contributing skeletal
elements to modern table refuse (see Table 18)

	Sheep	Pig	Rabbit	Cattle
Total identified(n)	155	61	64	12
Grouped elements	%	%	%	%
Head[1]	–	–	–	–
Foot[2]	10	67	–	–
Body[3]	90	33	100	100
Individual elements				
Mandible	–	–	–	–
Loose teeth	–	–	–	–
Vertebrae	48	20	69	100[5]
Small bones[4]	10	15	–	–
Metapodials	–	26	–	–

1 = Bones of cranium and lower jaws including any loose teeth
2 = All bones of metapodia including hock and carpal joints
3 = Ribs not counted in these results
4 = Small bones of hock and carpal joints
5 = Sacral and caudal or 'oxtail' vertebrae
From Wilson 1989a.

insignificant.

Data from bones very poorly represented the contribution of beef to the diet as proved by reference to its share by meat weight or cost of meat. Conversely, the bone data overrepresented the contribution of mutton, rabbit and to some extent, pork and bacon in my diet.

Where the representation of skeletal elements in the consumed meat was examined, as enabled by Table 19, bones of the heads of mammals were completely absent from the table refuse. Bones of the foot were absent or scarcely present, except abundantly from pig. Nearly all sheep, cattle and rabbit bones came from the rest of the body or main meat carcass and vertebrae were particularly abundant. Body bones from pig were less abundant. Fish vertebrae were very abundant and head elements were common.

Explanation of these results was straightforward. The bones present in the table refuse were entirely the result of the preparation of animal carcasses by butchery at the slaughterhouse, shop or supermarket. Almost all the beef was taken off its bones before it was sold, with the exception of the oxtail vertebrae which are less easily stripped of beef. By contrast, little mutton was removed from its bones before sale and carcasses were cut up quite extensively into joints. Pork was similarly prepared but where bacon was produced, the meat was taken off the bones. Little meat was taken off the rabbit and bird bones but some filleting of fish occurred.

Heads and feet of cattle, sheep, most pigs, rabbits and birds had always been removed from the carcasses and the bones utilised or disposed of elsewhere (brains and tongues were cut out and occasionally made available for sale, although not purchased by me). Pig butchery sometimes allowed the sale of the hock joint and trotters as these have some edible tissue on them and still may be regarded as a delicacy by a few people or as worth feeding to dogs.

This butchery pattern reflects quite well the factors which were considered earlier in chapters 5, 6 and 11 to determine broadly the nature and stages of butchery of animal carcasses and where they took place. In particular, the size of carcass tends to determine the extent to which it is cut up: large carcasses are extensively butchered, small ones scarcely.

In 20th century table refuse these economic and ergonomic factors are strongly evident and also are apparent in the formation of medieval waste debris although this rationale of meat butchery is less expected of prehistoric cultures. Use and value of offal products like tripe and sweetbreads must differ, being highly esteemed in many cultures where production and consumption of animals is mainly at subsistence level and not often at the prodigious, efficient but paradoxically sometimes wasteful scale of modern animal husbandry and butchery where the consumption of meat is taken for granted.

It has been possible to recognise the operation of similar economic butchery factors at medieval sites, particularly Hardings Field manor, although it must be remembered that this was a rural site and therefore butchery of animals on site was unlikely to have been carried out by fulltime butchers. Also to be noted is that some manor food, certainly seafish and shellfish, appears purchased via urban social organisation. Butchery, especially of smaller carcasses, as probably carried out in the manor kitchen, would have produced more waste than butchery in my flat kitchen although the manor 'waste' may have been utilised in some ways, e.g. to feed pets.

Such economic and ergonomic factors operated as far back as Roman times, for example in the baths of Caerleon, Gwent, Wales, where comparable bones of sheep and fowl from bathside snacks accumulated in the drains (O'Connor 1986). Further back, in our Iron Age settlements, the bone patterns might be explained by similar economic factors. Halstead and others (1978) thought this for the site at Wendens Ambo, Essex, but distinctive debris has as yet not satisfactorily been disentangled from the obscure mixtures of bones brought about by rubbish clearance and scavenging.

PART IV

ABSTRACTION AND APPLICATION OF GENERAL PRINCIPLES

......spatial and contextual data are important to many analytical problems, and may become important to new ones as the volume of neotaphonomic data increases. (Lyman 1994, 415).

[Explanation] ......can produce a dangerous situation. On the one hand it becomes imperative that accounts are not ethnocentric and do not merely confirm our prejudices and predilections (i.e. superiority of a scientific orientation in the world). On the other, if we resign ourselves to the view that every culture is different and provides a coherent and finite province of meaning, then we are dangerously close to a doctrine of cultural relativism...... (Moore 1982, 75).

......The time seems right to apply spatial analysis...... in the investigation of global questions. For example, instead of asking "How were space and activities organised at Site X?"..... it would probably be as important to ask "How was space organised and perceived among pleistocene hunter–gatherers?......

In short spatial analysis should be applied within a broader framework than has been the case so far. After all the primary goal of archaeology is to explain the development of mankind on a global scale (Blankholm 1991, 48–49).

Chapter 13

Concise Modelling: Description, Interpretation and Explanation

During 1990, concerned by the slowness of the publication of bone reports dealing with spatial patterning and bothered by the slow progress of general knowledge and approaches to writing reports, I expressed these frustrations within the profession of archaeology. Literature in this field was reviewed (less fully than given in chapter 1) and compared to unpublished work in the Upper Thames Valley which provided the means by which published bone distributions, especially feature type differences, could be better understood. This paper was read at an Association for Environmental Archaeology conference in Cambridge which dealt with the working relationship between site excavators and specialists like myself (Wilson 1994).

The subsidiary aim of the paper was to lay out a descriptive and causal model of spatial patterning of bones and, where known, artefacts on sites. Here my account is shortened by omitting most published and unpublished references to work already described in this book.

–0–

The first part of the model was purely a description of spatial findings to date.

As expected, greatest accumulations and densities of bones were found toward the centre of settlements and less toward the periphery. Typically, bone concentrations were associated with houses and hearths on less structurally differentiated sites like undefended rural Iron Age settlements (hillforts were less well documented in this respect). The spatial locations of houses and hearths on site seemed to determine much of the variability of the bone spread. A small circle of houses mainly preserved the central clustering of bone debris; a larger circle of houses tended to produce a ring of concentrated material surrounding an emptier central area.

Where buildings of later period differed in form and size, domestic buildings or rooms appeared associated with greater concentrations of bones than other parts of living quarters or farm buildings. At Hardings Field the greatest concentration of bones lay in rooms between the main hall and the kitchen.

Dense debris appeared associated with certain types of feature, particularly but not invariably pits and house gullies. Sizeable ditches, especially enclosure, trackway or field ditches, appeared less associated with dense bone scatters. At Mingies Ditch four–post structures were much less asssociated with bones than hearths and houses.

Bone spreads fell into three main categories: burnt debris; coarse debris, typically of cattle and horse bones; and medium and fine or small debris where bones of sheep, pig and sometimes smaller species predominated. 'Coarse' and 'fine' were relative and crude descriptions of bone aggregations but were very useful units of site analysis. Spreads of coarse and fine debris were found at sites of all periods and usually independently of the variable representation of individual species which appears largely determined by cultural factors.

On Iron Age sites medium fine and burnt debris were often associated with hearths and houses and to some extent with pits (also see Holmes 1993). At later sites, typically showing greater organisational differentiation, medium fine bones were associated with village houses (Harcourt 1986), farmhouses (including Halstead et al 1978 and Sadler 1990), domestic quarters and rooms, particularly where internal floor deposits survived. Medieval urban rubbish pits adjacent to houses also could contain relatively fine debris. Spreads of burnt bones at later sites were more diffuse and less obviously associated with hearths, except where these were better preserved (Sadler 1990).

Coarse debris occurred amongst finer stuff but predominated outside concentrations of medium fine and burnt bones. Coarse debris characterised external areas and contexts like ditches away from houses and hearths and characterised the periphery of settlements, rural and urban. There was considerable variability in this patterning, especially on urban sites where deposits of coarse debris might alternate with those of fine debris and according to the settlement layout and property structure. Coarse debris also appeared characteristic of building construction and demolition deposits and of site abandonment. Coarse debris was less associated with burnt bones, even on a mesolithic site (Wilson unpub. h) but not always.

At Mingies Ditch medium fine and burnt bones were closely associated with the bulk of the pottery and the few worked bones. Coarse debris was less well associated with these artefacts. Such relationships were not well explored at other British sites (although see Halstead et al 1978, Bradley & Fulford 1980 and Hill 1995) but advances in understanding have been made elsewhere by studies of post–medieval deposition (South 1977 and other period deposition (Rapson & Todd 1992) in the USA and at the Mesopotamian site of Abu Salabikh, Iraq (Mathews & Postgate 1990).

–0–

The second stage of the model was interpretative.

Size of bones, crudely related to both animal size and fragment size, was positively associated with increasing distance from centres of major bone and pottery concentrations. At Mingies Ditch the central–peripheral ranking of bone category accumulations was sheep, pig, cattle, horse and bones larger than 10cm in size. A small sample of dog bones indicated a more complicated bimodal distribution of species bones.

There was therefore a trend for bones to be distributed radially according to increasing size and decreasing density from centres of bone concentrations. In other words there were concentric or quasiconcentric zones of bone density and bone and fragment size. Where multiple bone concentrations occurred there was an interaction, often aggregative, of bone zone densities and this had to be allowed for in mapping and modelling. Such generalisation implied that the distribution of bones occured largely independently of types of feature outside hearths and houses. Where features of any type occurred close to houses and hearths medium fine, burnt and potsherd debris would tend to accumulate within them. Coarse and unburnt debris would tend to accumulate in more distant features, regardless of their type.

The extent of these accumulations varied, extending radially over scores of metres from the centre of sites, and thus over thousands of square metres of settlement, but at Mingies Ditch and Hardings Field most surviving debris appeared to have accumulated within 15 m of each domestic focal centre. Medium fine debris appeared more widely spread at Barton Court Farm. At Mingies Ditch domestic foci included internal hearths as well as external ones and there was a tendency for debris to accumulate outside the houses as if rubbish had been excluded from the first 5 m radius of the internal hearths. Comparable evidence occurred at Watkins Farm. Quantitative cultural variability in the concentric spread of debris was expected.

It was wondered if this work might be close to enunciating the kind of generalisations about the spatial distribution of bones and artefacts that behavioural and sampling theorists asserted or implied, during the 1970s, were possible to discover. Admittedly these regularities were scarcely of atom smashing scientific impact – one sceptic has scathingly referred to comparable instances as 'Mickey Mouse laws'. Minor regularities or not, they were trends applicable not just to rural and urban sites spanning four successive cultures and to modern experimental samples in the Upper Thames Valley, but possibly comparable to patterns at other sites, nationally and world-wide.

Spatial patterning could be described further at medieval and post-medieval sites where social differentiation and specialisation were more readily recognised in the archaeological record and bone preservation was better than on prehistoric sites. Among the small and fine debris in internal contexts, the representation of skeletal elements, especially vertebrae, of the main meat carcass of species like sheep, rabbit and domestic fowl was greater than in external contexts where foot and cranial elements were better represented. For sheep the pattern was repeated slightly differently at urban sites where most pit groups were closer to internal contexts in their species and elemental representation, while other external and sometimes peripheral settlement deposits contained high percentages of foot or cranial bones of sheep. The latter deposits were broadly associated with other specialised and peripheral deposits of cattle horncores and probably crania of older cattle and sometimes foot bones. In central areas most cattle elements were usually well mixed and widely dispersed except on late and post-medieval urban sites where cranial bones of calves stood out. With pig, foot and head elements were well represented among the fine debris. Greater documentation of such spatial patterning was required.

–0–

The third stage of the model concerned explanations of spatial patterning.

Despite objections by Hodder (1982b, 1985a and b and 1989 but see 1992, 83–86) and others, the general methodological orientation of processual archaeology substantiated by Bruce Schiffer, but perhaps harking back to the ideas of Heraclitus, appeared the simplest to adopt. A broad ecological explanatory context could be applied to the patterning of bones as ecofacts but less readily and less completely to spatial patterns of bones as artefactual debris alone. For at first, considering the apparent cross cultural universality of spatial patterns, a–cultural explanations seemed required, that is explanations independent of the fluctuating characteristics of individual symbolic and value ideal systems of Iron Age, Roman, Saxon, medieval and industrial cultures. These 'cultures' had been much discussed but less well defined where the fields of archaeological ecology and cultural archaeology overlapped. For example, the traditional treatment of materials like coins and pottery of successive cultures in any given region appeared to be a discussion of 'high' cultures, rather like the preoccupation of earlier historians with royalty, religious and mercantile classes, the history of art, and far less a concern with the relative continuity of human ecology that sustained them.

At this point of discussion the paradigmatic can of methodological worms and philosophical position-taking of different types of scientists and archaeologists could scarcely be opened. My aim was to avoid an over-rigid categorisation of human nature and archaeological intent and to refer back to the compromising 'ecocultural' context of discussion defined in Chapter 2. Involvement of environmentalists with examining ecocultural processes was, of course, well attested though few used the word yet.

Then discussion moved on to the processes relevant to the interpretation and explanation of spatial patterns of bones and sherds.

First there was the question of sampling error. Use of data from hand-picked bone collections in the analysis of the above sites might be thought suspect due to demonstrable limited recovery of small bones by sieving (Payne 1972b and Wilson, Bramwell & Wheeler 1979), especially in peripheral areas where features were large or appeared less interesting, and therefore excavated less well.

Some data from soil sieving at Mount Farm and Hardings Field indicate that, although a proportion of smaller bones are missed during the collection of hand-picked samples, the percentage trends of coarse and fine debris are still recognisable in both sieved and hand–picked bone groups from the same features (chapters 6 and 7). Thus the differences observed in the spread of bone debris between central and peripheral areas of sites appear unlikely to be greatly affected by differential recovery.

The limited evidence and provisional conclusions drawn from sieving work appear supported by other general refutation of the argument of poor recovery of smaller bones in large features and peripheral areas. At Barton Court Farm most of the bones were collected from sizeable ditches and the palisade ditch of the inner area was deeper and wider than the outermost ditches yet the bones recovered from these features show the opposite trend to that which would be expected from the differential recovery hypothesis. At Mingies Ditch the pattern of results from the central to peripheral spread of bones is seen to be established before results from the large enclosure ditches are taken into account. Furthermore the enclosure ditches there, including the entranceway, show a more complicated pattern of bone debris instead of a simple spread of coarse debris as would be expected. Other factors appear more important than differential recovery.

Then consideration should be given to where an extensive and featureless layer of deposition occurred in the central area at Mingies Ditch and thus, where recovery of bones ought to have been poor, this large layer actually yielded large numbers and high percentages of medium size debris. Similarly, at Claydon Pike where the featureless layer of deposition covering and concealing the underlying features was far more extensive than the layer at Mingies Ditch, the pattern of coarse and fine debris recovered is more complicated than would be expected by the differential recovery hypothesis. Clustering of similar results in adjacent grid squares rather than random variation and gradation is evident and appears related most to locations of most buildings and or domestic activity. There is a possiblity that retrieval of bones from ditches on this site would be poorer than from other smaller features but results from these features were not part of the analysis of results from the layer. Also, much of the excavation of the layer appears to have been done blind, that is with limited knowledge of features such as ditches below. Thus diggers could hardly have anticipated which parts of the layer and the site would be of greatest interest and attract more intensive bone retrieval than other parts. Although an unploughed layer of deposition covering deep features was lacking at Mount Farm, similar argument could be advanced for differences in bone distribution between northern and southern areas where the layout of features (Fig. 11) did not suggest areas of greater digging interest than others.

Second, there was the issue of bone preservation or degradation. It was chiefly relevant because it destroyed information about spatial activity in past ecocultures. Differential effects of bone preservation did not appear to explain the overall patterning of bones on sites (chapter 10). Qualitatively at least, patterning of species bones of common domestic animals appeared largely unaffected by bone degradation, a finding supported by Mark Maltby (pers.

comm.).

Third, there was the process of scavenging action. Decomposers, like dogs, foxes and birds, disarticulated, destroyed and scattered bones from naturally dying carcasses, from butchered remains, and from cooked bone refuse. Typically, unconsumed bone waste was scattered outward from its source, larger elements and fragments farther than smaller debris.

Fourth, there was the process of 'rubbish' (detritus might be a more neutral term) clearance and dumping. Ecocultural trophic ('feeding') processes were not always exploitatively efficient and left waste which sometimes accumulated sufficiently to interfere with the efficacy of other frequent or important site activities, especially domestic functioning – chiefly eating, cooking and food preparation including butchery. Significant rubbish in activity areas had to be removed. Large items and large quantities of smaller waste were cleared from intensively used areas, particularly domestic ones around internal and external hearths. Items larger than 9 cm were prone to 'rubbish' disposal while smaller items were frequently left behind (Rathje 1979, 9–10) although Schiffer (1980, 280–81 and 1983, 679–80) and his students among the Nacirema (sic) indicate that items as small as 3 cm may frequently be moved.

Fifth, there was the complicated business of carcass utilisation, butchery specialisation and location. Butchery was subject to similar constraints of exploitative efficiency in the organisation of human activity in space. Multiple need satisfaction in eating as close as possible to fires where food was cooked took central precedence over the butchery of animal carcasses. However the butchery and cooking of small carcasses and meat joints could be integrated better with other food preparation and other pressing activities in the domestic area than could the butchery of large carcasses.

Thus large carcasses of sheep and cattle sized animals tended to be disjointed (especially sheep and pigs) and or deboned (especially cattle and horse) on the periphery of domestic areas. Smaller carcasses of rabbits, birds and fish tended to be butchered less and nearer the hearth and cooked relatively intact.

Bones of the small animals and of meat joints of larger animals, including pig trotters and heads, survived as cooked meal or table refuse, and were a good indicator of eating areas and scullery action in rooms and buildings or near them. Kitchen refuse appeared characterised by leg and head elements from small animals or some elements from medium sized carcasses e.g. calf head bones – perhaps those boiled for brawn. On urban sites butchers' refuse appeared indicated by some medium–sized waste like halved sheep skulls. Refuse of slaughterhouses and associated fellmongery trades displayed foot and head elements of larger animals and other bones of largest animals and sometimes bones of species like horse not commonly eaten by man. Additional variability in butchery deposits was to be expected, e.g. for pig where pork was prepared for preservation or kept fresh for direct consumption. These types of refuse were scarcely evident for less urbanised, less specialised, less intensive, and less productive divisions of human labour and other resources at sites, especially where settlements were populated by small numbers of people or by people participating in a subsistence economy.

–0–

Then it seemed worth considering the wider meaning of these site processes. Butchery, detritus clearance and scavenging all interactively distributed and redistributed ecocultural detritus, the smaller and finer debris remaining centrally and greater proportions of coarse debris being left peripherally. Waste originally accumulated as a result of the compaction of crucial human practices of food preparation, cooking and eating into as small a space as possible, except where material structures and utensils or status display dictated greater spacing of activities like feasting. At certain small settlements detritus might be ignored or symbolically and ritually structured, as shown by the works of Hodder (1982a) and Moore (1981 and 1982) in Kenya and Sudan and of Bulmer (1976) in New Guinea. Where sufficient waste built up at large settlements, especially towns and cities, butchery and cleaning practices would become even more spatially differentiated so that trade and industrial processes less connected with feeding people would often be displaced toward the edge of settlements. Thus space at settlement centres was used more efficiently and less offence was caused by large quantities of guts, hides and bones being stored, processed or disposed of. Domestic refuse might also be removed systematically. In towns like medieval Oxford some of these changes were brought about through enacting controlling laws. Nonetheless, despite these regulatory trends, social differences, economic and other exploitative intensification like war, and other factors brought about further conceptual and behavioural diversity and therefore depositional variability.

Over aeons the essentially ecological processing of producers (i.e. plants) and consuming herbivores, carnivores and scavengers was substantially altered by hominids and humans into a complex combination of food–growing, hunter–gathering, animal husbandry and multi–faceted food consumption. The 'consumer' sector of the human role in community ecology often remained psychologically conservative but with a new affective component contained in overall need satisfaction and survival.

The additional component was the cultural function of the domestic fire. It was relevant to the discussion because the possession of fire probably assisted in the displacement of human feeding from the immediate sources of food to the somewhat safer and more satisfying consumption of food and drink close to the fireplace. Significance of the adoption of fire had been remarked on previously (e. g. Kroll & Isaac 1984, 7) but the centrality of cooking and eating to human organisation from hunter–gatherers to complex urban entities was probably what characterised the continuity of radial or concentric patterning of bones and other artefacts from prehistoric times to the industrial era in England and elsewhere.

Before the taming of fire, scavenging and probably detritus clearance and differential butchery processes occurred but perhaps would be less evident depositionally in the absence of the attractions of hearths which would focus and structure deposition of bones and artefacts. Change in these activities from early man to 20th century peoples seemed most evident in the increasing degree of individual and social self–differentiation in physical resource exploitation and in human reorganisation resulting from need and want multiplication in different cultures. These spatial and temporal changes were manifested in differences, alterations and therefore complexity of bone patterning in the archaeological record.

At some places and stages of human evolution, differentiation between bone accumulations appeared more recognisable than at others, e.g. in Roman and post–medieval urban deposits. But the spatial setting of most deposits and their universal significance in relation to human identity had been largely obscured by the limitations of excavation, environmental analysis and publication.

Chapter 14

Intercultural Differences in Maps of Bone Spreads

Having elaborated on the excavations which have allowed the building of an interpretive and explanatory model based on spatial patterning of bones, it is now worth considering how regular or variable the spatial pattern is from one cultural instance of it to another. Accordingly, the four major rural sites of Barton Court Farm, Mingies Ditch, Claydon Pike and Hardings Field, and their bone patterning (percentage of sheep and pig bones) have been compared at the same map scale in Fig. 28. The map of Oxford bone debris has not been added to the comparison since, first, the excavations in the town are located and mapped at a different order of magnitude than the rural sites given. Second, the contour mapping of the bone debris of Oxford is estimated from widely scattered sample bone groups rather than as being quantified like the retrieved debris recorded at the smaller but relatively complete rural excavations.

It is still difficult to write with precision in making any quantitative comparison of site bone spreads of different period and culture. Fig. 28 only too plainly shows the different methods by which the bone spreads have been mapped. The maps differ in the degree in which occupation layers survived above the level of other site features. At Barton Court Farm the occupation layers had been largely ploughed out. Elsewhere they survived better.

Then the maps differ due to the varying rigour of the spatial location of bones within occupation layers or deep features. At Barton Court Farm, the earliest dug site, bone groups from deep features could only be located approximately within the site plan and feature record. By contrast, at Mingies Ditch, bones and other finds could be located and recorded to within 2 m of their actual find spots. Thus it became possible to incorporate finds from shallow and deep features to provide bone data for any sampling based on the 2 m grid system.

Precision of recording and location of bones in the occupation debris at Claydon Pike and Hardings Field fell between the standards set at Barton Court Farm and Mingies Ditch. Not only were the four excavations carried out by three different site directors but the priorities of site excavation differed according to the varying preconceptions and problems of excavating sites of different cultural period.

By way of explaining the variable methodology above, prehistoric sites generally appear to receive much closer attention in the recording of settlement debris; indeed Palaeolithic excavators might be horrified at the lack of precision of the bone records above. The divergence in recording partly reflects the frequent paucity of finds and structural evidence at frequently shallow early prehistoric sites but, more importantly, is a reflection of the abundance of site debris at the often larger and more intensively occupied settlements of historic and late prehistoric eras. Excavators of Roman, Saxon and medieval settlements tend to sacrifice or compromise on the desirability of accurate positional recording of thousands of finds, particularly of bones, on deep town sites when there is a need to excavate quickly and to record complex stratigraphy as well as possible within the usual constraint of limited funds.

Lastly the differences in mapping precision reflect the initial inexperience but growing awareness of archaeologists in getting to grips with both old and new excavation problems, especially in digging large sites and improving professional standards of work. The advance to attain numeracy and scientific requirements are part of the urge of archaeologists towards their own professional competence.

The adoption and utilization of computers in archaeology has now become almost routine but there have been severe limitations of software appropriate to spatial analysis. It is noticeable that computing has not made many satisfactory contributions to the mapping and interpretation of bone debris in space (but see Ferring 1984 and Whallon 1984).

Regional spatial analysis was very much a matter of the use of calculator, pen and paper. In any case, bearing in mind the complexity of archaeological phenomena, it seemed better to restrict numerical work to investigating overall parameters using simple calculations and not attempting an elaborate and possibly inappropriate analysis.

Hot on my methodological heels and around the mid 1980s, however, better statistical, wider mathematical and computational methods were brought in, e.g. the work of Christopher Carr (1984 and 1985), that gathered under the editorship of Harold Hietala (1984a) and, more recently, the effort of Hans Peter Blankholm (1991). These came largely too late to influence my site work. Besides, these methods, like k–means analysis, tend to deal with finds which have been precisely recorded in space. With the exception of papers on cell frequency recording, by Johnson (1984), Spurling and Hayden (1984) and Cribb (1991), few new techniques appeared to consider bone groups collected within the basic square units of a site grid system.

–0–

Having outlined some of the limitations of method in the spatial investigation of the Upper Thames Valley settlements, and having discussed why the site bone spread spatial representations vary in Fig. 28, one can then ask whether there is sufficient variation in the distributions of mapped bones that might be related to cultural differences rather than ecocultural similarities in scavenging, detritus clearance and butchery practices?

The question appears unanswerable. Although the general trends of decreasing amounts of medium coarse debris at greater distances away from the centres of domestic activity are evident, site variation or outright differences between the spread of debris at sites are not convincingly evident. And,

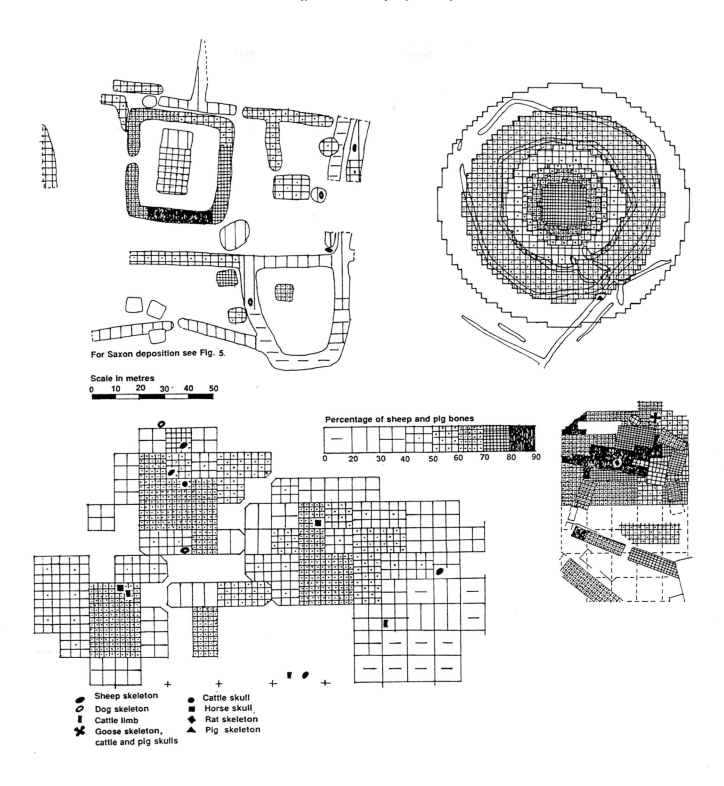

For Saxon deposition see Fig. 5.

Scale in metres
0   10   20   30   40   50

Percentage of sheep and pig bones
0   20   30   40   50   60   70   80   90

- Sheep skeleton
- Dog skeleton
- Cattle limb
- Goose skeleton, cattle and pig skulls
- Cattle skull
- Horse skull
- Rat skeleton
- Pig skeleton

Fig. 28. Comparison of the distribution of medium sized bone debris (percentage of sheep and pig bones and articulated remains at four regional sites, all drawn at the same scale.

75

since the floor level deposition in the farmhouse at Barton Court Farm was completely destroyed long before excavation, there is no internal house deposit standard (percentage of sheep and pig bones), apart from demolition debris, to compare with the known deposits of site refuse (the destroyed deposit layers may also mean that the medium and small animal species are underrepresented among the bones recovered from the site).

The highest concentration of sheep and pig bones differs from site to site. Percentages of the above species bones combined are highest at Hardings Field and lowest at Claydon Pike. These differences indicate genuine cultural differences between rural settlements of different period and culture, for instance an appreciable consumption of pig meat at Hardings Field should be noted, but the determining causality is difficult to state – yet see Chapter 15. In brief at present we have come to the limits of being able to interpret intersite differences in the spreads of settlement bones.

All that has been described in these mapping studies are general trends of bone distributions. They can be interpreted to give an understanding of the general and qualitative cultural and natural processes which went on at settlements but the results can rarely be interpreted precisely enough to determine the quantitative contribution of each cultural or natural process to the observed bone pattern.

Also we must acknowledge the generality of the cumulative patterns that have been discussed. Often at smaller sites of sparser or complicated bone information, the general pattern of debris can not be found with any confidence even though intuitively I think we know a lot about how the bone distribution probably came about. An example of this is to be found in my longish report on the Middle Iron Age settlement on the Lechlade site adjacent to the Claydon Pike late Iron Age and Romano–British settlement (Wilson unpub. i).

Chapter 15

Symbolic Variations on a Spatial Theme

Circumstances have changed a great deal since I embarked on British archaeology during 1973. Not only has there been considerable change in the organisational conditions under which archaeological work is entered upon but there has been much alteration in the attitudes of archaeologists toward the theory of their subject.

Other archaeologists had the benefit and the hindrance of being trained in archaeological tradition and correlated ethos. By contrast, those having certain advantages of being trained in both natural and social sciences, could make a contribution to work on biological remains and their deposition without being weighed down by the mainstream of traditional orientations and practical issues in digging and reporting of sites.

Admittedly I set out with similar assumptions and presumptions to other similarly recruited environmentalists in possessing knowledge and confidence in scientific method but mainly paid attention to the immediate practicalities of coping with the backlog of bone collections on which to write reports. Much basic work had to be done in getting reports written and any criticism and deficiencies of the philosophy of science seemed trivial by contrast.

As demonstrated in this book, the chronology of the published literature bears some correspondence to the programme of spatial work in the Upper Thames Valley but this attention neglected other fields, particularly, the theoretical side of mainstream archaeology. What was known had been gleaned from bone reports, specialist courses and conferences with other environmentalists and archaeologists.

Incredibly perhaps, I was not very familiar with the work of Binford on bones. When made aware of his *Nunamiut archaeology*, (Binford 1978b) I skimmed through the book seeking matters relevant to my immediate work. When the text I was looking for was to be found in *Pursuit of the past* (Binford 1983), his other work was paid less attention, probably because the American literature on bones was usually less relevant than keeping up to date in the British literature which mostly focussed on post–Mesolithic sites rather than on the problems of interpreting the evidence of the Palaeolithic.

Another arena of the literature I paid minimal attention to was the somewhat later publications of Ian Hodder, particularly during 1982 when both *Symbols in action and Structural archaeology* appeared. Catching up on the numerous publications of Hodder was, like the reading of Binford, delayed largely until the 1990s when I had greater time at leisure to assimilate the wider perspectives of archaeological theory.

Other theorists also have stated their ideas. In the critique of Michael Shanks and Christopher Tilley, scientific method does not emerge satisfactorily due to their implicating it as time–biased, reductionist, essentialist and ethnocentric (imbued with the ideas and values of capitalism) in its intent and content (Shanks & Tilley 1987a and b). Others joined the onslaught on environmental archaeology (e.g. Thomas 1990). Consequently the methods, results and conclusions of spatial analysis are impugned and devalued. Ideological issues of this kind are best resolved separately in properly addressed books and papers (O'Connor 1991, Lloyd 1993, Yoffee & Sherratt 1993 and Wilson 1995). Here, as long as my methodology has, and continues, to reveal material patterning and reasonable, albeit provisional, interpretations and explanations, my approach to archaeology is still manifestly scientific even if it is erratic or inconsistent in practice due to culturebound and reflexive difficulties of interpreting archaeological materials.

Nontheless, where interesting and valuable insights into symbolic and structural anthropology and archaeology concerning bones have been uncovered by Hodder and others, I have welcomed them, even if there are problems with their application to excavated bones and their context. All in all, the best insights of the symbolic kind have been regrettably few though notably provided concerning the life of the Nuba in the Sudan as developed in the text of *Symbols in action* (Hodder 1982a, 154–61, 190–93 and 215–6) and of the Kalam in New Guinea (Bulmer 1976). Those unfamiliar with these references are urged to read the noted pages fully.

The case of the Nuba is particularly interesting. At their settlements, although some bone debris appears disposed of without ceremony, it being thrown outside the enclosures or compounds to its destruction by dogs, there is a tendency to separate the bones of cattle from those of pigs in social activities ranging from the display of certain skeletal elements to the segregation of bones of different species into distinctive caches or other deposits. Some cranial elements are retained within the house compounds and often built into the walls of granaries. Within three Nuba tribes there is some preference for either pig or cattle (or goat) skulls and mandibles to be used in this display. Elsewhere, where there is a risk of the mixing of bones of the two main species, they are collected up and deposited in separate groups at some distance outside the house compounds. The Kalam exhibit similar behaviour in displaying hunting trophies in house walls and in hanging up bone waste in trees and shrubs.

Hodder explained the bone distribution by the conceptual structure of the minds of Nuba tribespeople. For example, among the Mesakin Qisar people, pigs, and therefore their bones, are associated with women and pollution while cattle, and their bones, are associated with men and cultural purity. To avoid pollution of male entities it becomes necessary to separate cattle bones from those of pig. The behavioural detail in the expression of the conceptual structures of different tribes is varied and more intricate than described above but need not be reiterated here.

Interestingly, it was then argued that the bones at hypothetically excavated Nuba settlements and graveyards could be recognised as symbolicaly structured, providing that appropriate conceptual models were used, being formulated and based on the deduction of general structural oppositions, such as clean/dirty, life/death, and male/female, from the archaeological remains.

Various responses to the anthropological discoveries of Hodder appear useful. One first notes the broad resemblence of central and peripheral types of Nuba bone debris to the cross cultural pattern of coarse and medium sized debris observed at British sites. Ironically the culturally relative symbolic explanation that Hodder elucidated from the Nuba activities could in principle explain the cross cultural pattern although it would not be the same explanation as other peoples might offer! In other words, the symbolism specific to the Mesakin Qisar, along with other emic, i.e. insider, explanations of bone detritus of other cultures, might be fitted within the generalities of the broadly functionalist explanations of the model of bone patterning put forward so far. One might speculate about the conscious and unconscious ways in which bone detritus is recognised, categorised, symbolised and even reordered by different peoples above the mundane mechanisms of bone dispersal at most sites.

Without getting further into the speculative ramifications of explaining the above (through lack of other good bony anthropological examples), it seems more useful to ask whether the species bone deposits made by the Mesakin Qisar would be recognisable in the cross cultural patterning of excavated detritus? The question assumes that peripheral and central accumulations and caches of Nuba animal bones would be disturbed, broken, scattered and mixed by house demolition, scavenging, decay and other post-depositional processes.

According to the model, cattle bones around the Mesakin Qisar settlement periphery would not be outstanding in the cultural patterning of site bones and no special meaning would be given to their presence. Bones of pig spread peripherally and abundantly could be sufficiently prominent in, and different to, the expected cross cultural pattern that questions of their species significance would be asked.

Pig bones among crumbled houses, granaries and their immediate vicinity would not stand out immediately, unless pig head debris was so abundant as to highlight the paucity of other elements of pig carcasses in the central area. Conversely, although it does not occur at Mesakin Qisar settlements, if cattle bones, particularly head elements, occurred in some abundance in the central areas of other Nuba compounds, one would be inclined to argue that its presence was significantly different from the cross cultural pattern. Thus only part of any symbolic structuring of the bones at Nuba settlements would stand out against the normally expected pattern of excavated bones.

A second response to examining the pattern of debris at British settlements is to ask whether models of symbolic structuring of the kind intuited by Hodder and others could apply to British bone distributions? The answer is 'Possibly.' as he argued applied to Neolithic sites in the Orkney Islands (Hodder 1982, 218–19). Yet where the intrasite spatial pattern of bones has been mapped systematically and has been found to display some consistency from culture to culture in Britain, the probability that the deposition of most bones was strongly structured symbolically appears quite low. One outcome of scientific rationale is that if bones were so structured, the symbolism and conceptual structure involved presumably would be similar from site to site, e.g. based on 'cattle/horse to the exterior; pig/sheep to the interior', rather than explained less parsimoniously by the different conceptual systems of each culture. Patterning of sites from Iron Age to Post-medieval periods appear better explained largely by functional or natural considerations rather than by symbolic action or reaction.

An example for discussion of symbolic action is in the great abundance of pig bones (39%) at the manor of Hardings Field although they mainly fell within the expected central zone of normal spatial patterning. While this abundant presence is undoubtedly a reflection of the status and of dietary prosperity of the occupying Barentin family, one can only see pig as being a weak and possibly subconscious symbol with regard to any deliberate deposition of the bones and therefore was a minor part of medieval conceptions of the processes of rubbish clearance, butchery and scavenging. In terms of dietary appreciation, however, pig, pork and bacon figured much more prominently in medieval symbolism but this appears largely unrelated to the spatial patterning of bones, unless the head debris of pig in the manorhouse is held to have been symbolically significant and intentionally retained within the walls. Bone assemblage composition at this site appears mainly linked to a complex of other economic, ecological and social factors.

When other British site collections are examined from the symbolic viewpoint, only a few exceptions displaying distinctive components stand out where general detritus spreads are ruminated over, even where other criteria point to symbolic and ritual activities characterising bony deposits. One excellent case is demonstrated for the Uley Hill Roman temples in Gloucestershire where both goat and chicken bones occurred abundantly in the general spread of detritus around the buildings and where the contemporary site iconography of these two species indicates a strong religious link and symbolism in the presence of the bones of these animals (Ellison 1981 and Levitan 1993).

Another conceivable exception to the disappointing revelation of symbolic action yielded by bones at British sites is the presence of horse bones and sometimes their association with dog bones in deposits, notably the 18th-century one at the Witney palace, Oxfordshire (Wilson & Edwards 1993). Such deposits appear essentially peripheral in character and are nondomestic in origin. Yet, although strong symbolic significance in early and recent British cultures is and was attached to both horse and dog, the actual deposition of horse bones at the palace appears only indirectly related, and even opposed, to the overt public symbolism and sentiment concerning the species (Edwards 1987) and was more directly related to opportunist economic exploitation of worn out and injured horses for skins and for meat to feed hunting and pet dogs during the post–medieval period. Criteria of value rather than symbolism explain the post–medieval accumulations of horse and dog bones (Wilson & Edwards 1993).

–0–

Where the location of more complete and less degraded bones, i.e. the distribution of part or complete animal skeletons, is considered, there is renewed hope of identifying some past symbolic or ritual activity. Maltby (1985b, 49–74) has discussed this possibility well.

Elsewhere in the literature a number of authors have noted the prevalence of articulated bones and skulls of animals in Iron Age pits, particularly at Danebury hillfort, Hampshire. These bones have been termed 'special deposits' and it has been argued that they were ritually deposited (Cunliffe 1983 and 1992, Grant 1984, Wait 1985 and Hill 1995). Yet such bone debris is found in features of other type and of contemporary and later periods and less ritual significance can be read into the pit burials unless much stronger material associations or religious contexts can be argued for individual deposits or unless it is shown that the bones have been formally positioned in a recognisable way (Wilson 1992).

Spatial location of such unusual deposits has rarely been discussed although at Barton Court Farm it was noted that the location of sheep burials lay toward the site periphery while some dog burials lay around the farmhouse and others were scattered away from it. This pattern reflects trends elsewhere. Generally, sheep skeletons are not uncommon at sites and tend to lie peripherally, perhaps within small ditched enclosures, and reflect the location of husbandry practices and the vulnerablity of sheep to diseases. Dog skeletons too are quite common at sites, and their site distribution is widespread in location and may reflect their diverse ecocultural roles as scavengers, work animals and pets. By contrast, few whole cattle skeletons have been found at Thames Valley sites and no pattern emerges, except that one burial of a butchered Roman cow at Smithsfield, Oxfordshire, occurred at the base of a square ditched enclosure similar to Gallic shrines, and may have been ritually deposited (Allen 1981 and Wilson 1992).

By way of analytical illustration, locations of burials of relatively complete skulls and articulated remains have been plotted amongst the surface spread at Claydon Pike, Fig. 28. Potentially, any of these remains might be ritual in origin. One line of relevant enquiry would be to compare them against their contrasting background of bone detritus. Intuition suggests that such burials of bones amongst peripheral locations and coarse debris would be less significant ritually in the functioning of the settlement (unless the burials were related to the marking of settlement boundaries). Most ritual activities might be expected to focus on areas of greatest farming activities, particularly

where their investment around buildings of greatest domesticity and fertility would appear symbolically important.

At Claydon Pike most of the articulated remains occur among coarse bone debris and thus were 'peripherally' located and are probably without ritual significance. However, several cattle and horse skulls were located in zones of medium fine debris in and around former buildings, appear out of place in terms of being normally categorised as coarse debris, and therefore may have been deliberately and ritually placed, e.g. as foundation deposits. Another convincing instance of this pattern is difficult to provide although remains of a horse were found next to the Romano–British farmhouse at Barton Court where the spread of medium sized debris would have been and, if of the same date, would indicate another 'out of place' deposit.

As mentioned in chapter 8, similar unusual deposits occurred at medieval Hardings Field, Fig. 18, but most were clustered in Room A5, the garderobe, where a background of coarse debris was more evident, e.g. among demolition debris in robber trenches, than elsewhere in the house. Thus the goose skeleton and skulls of cattle and pig did not appear out of place. Neither did a black rat skeleton amongst medium sized and small debris in the main hall. Locations of two part skeletons of cat were less well recorded but evidently neither was certainly linked to the building foundations. A puppy skeleton occurred in Room M. All the latter remains can at best be inconclusively connected with any ritual activities of this and later eras (Merrifield 1987).

It becomes evident that any ritual and symbolic burials of animals or their parts usually do not stand out at the majority of sites. Nevertheless, unmistakeable evidence of ritual activity in the symbolic manipulation of such bone remains occurs in the Romano–British interment singly of two dog skulls and one of sheep with three infant burials at Barton Court Farm (Miles 1986). Thus burials of skulls, like those noted at Claydon Pike, probably have more ritual significance than the depositional evidence elsewhere strictly illuminates.

While more may be made of such remains in other publications, some reservation here seems preferable. Nontheless we should encourage more anthropological studies like those of Hodder which open up broader vistas to both particulars and universalities of human behaviour involving bones. Recent contributions are contained under the editorship of Willis (1994).

Chapter 16

From the Oxford Blackfriars, back through Neolithic Monumental Sites, to Bone Spreads of Olduvai Hominids

Having deduced some of the spatial patterning of bones, postulating its causal processes, and briefly discussing the influence of cultural conceptual systems, it is natural to look about in the literature to see if the modelling throws further light on site interpretations.

An example among the settlements already examined is the smallish collection of bones from the Blackfriars site on the southern periphery of Oxford. A scatter of the usual animal bones were retrieved from many narrow trenches dug across the monastic site under the direction of George Lambrick. In one area, however, masses of fish bones were prominent in several layers and in a drain. Soil samples were sieved to provide an interesting group of mainly marine fish bones including many plates of sturgeon (Harman 1985 and Wilkinson 1985).

Since the percentage of cattle bones was higher than that among the bone assemblages elsewhere in the town, it was suggested initially that the Black friars ate a much higher proportion of beef than the secular inhabitants of Oxford, with the implication that the monastery was better able to afford the beef and fish than other townspeople.

With improved information now available from other town sites, the percentages of cattle and horse (not many horse bones are part of the coarse debris) bones used in the mapping of site debris indicate that the percentage of cattle bones at Blackfriars is not particularly unusual and occurs within the range of results from other sites of different type. Moreover, the town map shows that the Blackfriars percentage of cattle bones is typical of peripheral sites of the town.

Using the spatial model to investigate bone distributions, we can confidently accept that the fish bones were table or kitchen refuse and a good indication of monastic diet.

When the cattle bones are so considered, the model predicts they will be more numerous at the periphery of the settlement, i.e. of Oxford, due to the outward scattering of larger debris by scavengers and human rubbish clearance, and by the proximity of slaughtering places of the large animals which were redirected toward the town periphery as the town grew in size. Therefore some or much of the coarser refuse of cattle on the Blackfriars site probably originated from other town sources rather than from monastic tables, kitchens and slaughterhouses (Lambrick 1985).

Put simply, there is no reliable bone evidence to support any contention that the friars ate a lot of beef. Having understood the medieval butchery and market redistribution of carcass parts of cattle and other sizeable species, it is just too difficult to trace or estimate the amount of beef eaten by the monks or people elsewhere in Oxford unless documentary sources are found to help out.

–0–

It is worth turning to reconsider the bones of Ashville Trading Estate and Appleford Iron Age settlements since the results there stimulated the investigation of spatial patterning (chapter 3). Re-examination of the bone assemblages or their data is unlikely to yield any spatial patterning missed previously but at least the spatial model which was developed subsequently allows an understanding of why the percentages of different species bones came about in the pit versus ditch contrast.

Although similar pit versus ditch differences were found at other sites too (chapter 1), it should have become clear that feature type differences are secondary to the generation of bone debris by related activities occupying space (after all, bones were still distributed in recognisable patterns in space where certain types of features such as storage pits were absent). Therefore a consideration of where different types of features are located at settlements in relation to bone fragment producing activities is likely to explain feature type differences.

Using our model, we would predict that pits were often closer than 'ditches' to centres of Iron Age domestic activity because of the general preponderance of sheep and pig bones in pit groups. 'Ditch' groups are complicated in spatial terms since the group's feature sources of bones at Ashville included gullies surrounding houses as well as gullies and ditches farther away from houses and their internal domestic activity. Examination of settlement plans, e.g. Fig. 4, shows that the layout of features is often complicated but the general sense of my argument ought to be seen, for example, enclosure and field ditches will be located farther away from houses and domestic activities than the gullies and pits around houses.

Where such feature type differences are compared period by period, one can also detect species differences due to the different placement of features and related activities over time. At Ashville the middle period of Iron Age occupation consisted of the most concentrated activity and the pit group had the highest percentage of sheep and pig bones. However, since the periphery of the settlement was ill-defined by excavation, it is difficult to conclude for certain that domestic activities occurred 'centrally'.

According to this argument then, we can, in principle, understand the observed feature type differences by consideration of our model from a different view of it although at Ashville we can not actually check our supposition because the settlement plan is very incomplete.

This kind of discussion should make it clearer than ever why limited excavations of settlements may yield misleading collections of bones since there may be an additional bias in whether central or peripheral activity areas are excavated or sampled. If, however, the extent and nature of the settlement is broadly interpretable from cropmarks and well–placed trial and sampling trenches, then some allowance can be made in the discussion of results according to the spacing of the trenches and the type of debris in them.

–0–

Another site where our model of spatial bone distributions can be applied is the Abingdon Neolithic causewayed enclosure. All one need know about the site is that it was formed by two approximately concentric segmented ditches and probably by the use of the natural boundaries of two adjoining streams.

Interpretations of the bone detritus at the site differ. Leslie Cram (1982) and Michael Avery (1982) concluded that bones from the inner ditch were largely domestic refuse and infilled and levelled prior to the construction of the outer ditch. Richard Bradley (1986) queried this interpretation with arguments which are not strongly persuasive but suggested the inner ditch deposits were deposited intentionally, that is, not as casual waste disposal but deliberately structured symbolicly and ritually. In particular, this was argued because there was a difference in species abundance between the bony contents of the inner and outer ditches.

Although bones from the outer ditch section numbered only 39, cattle bones clearly predominated while a tooth constituted the only representation of pig (Case 1956): by contrast, pig bones made up 34% of the sizeable inner ditch deposits. Presence of pig bones there was implied to be special and symbolicly significant.

Yet if our cross cultural and cross time model of bone distribution is applied, coarse debris is expected from the outer ditch and less coarse debris is expected from the inner ditch. Thus the 79% or more of cattle bones from the outer ditch rests quite satisfactorily with the 58% of cattle bones from the inner ditch. This comparison appears valid regardless of whether the ditches are contemporary or of somewhat different date, and also confirms that site activity, but not necessarily ritual action, was focussed most in the inner area as Bradley's arguments indicated.

Our general model implies that the inner and outer ditch debris is basically domestic in origin. Larger bones radiated outward from the inner area by detritus clearance and scavenging, and,or came from the butchery of cattle in peripheral zones. There is little to indicate anything exceptional in the deposition of the bones, especially as Bradley had to draw on deposition at a more obvious ritual monument, an oval barrow nearby, to argue his case that inner ditch deposition was intentional. Obviously the debate rests on the quality of the excavation evidence.

The relative abundance of pig at the site appears best seen in the context of a relative absence of sheep bones at the site and other small sites in the region. Reasoning for this is ecological, it being argued that Neolithic grass pasture for sheep and cattle was not as widespread as previously believed (Barker & Webley 1978) and woodland or scrubland was moderately abundant and best suited the husbandry of pigs and cattle (Robinson & Wilson 1987, 34–36). Quite large numbers of the two species and some sheep were raised in the region and brought near the causewayed enclosure for slaughtering (of course the numbers selected need not have corresponded exactly to the species proportions in the populations at large). Cattle bones at the enclosure, especially indicate the boning out of meat occurring in the vicinity.

The possibility of feasting at causewayed enclosures, as signified by the presence of articulated remains was discussed and dismissed by Cram. Although the nature of Neolithic butchery is not well known, the presence of articulated remains should primarily be regarded as a result of butchery technique and also as a result of fortunate preservation and relatively quick burial of such remains. Whether feasting or other symbolic manipulation of available meat and bones was involved is a great deal less certain. Equally, the putative suggestion above that the bones appear 'domestic' in origin might be revised and a submodel of spatial and symbolically structured bone processes could be postulated (chapter 17). Nonetheless the only tangible evidence of symbolic and ritual behaviour at the Abingdon causewayed enclosure would depend on the strength of non osteological arguments that the building and operation of causewayed enclosures established a ritual context for site activities.

–0–

Another important site with interesting interpretations of results is the Neolithic and Beaker period enclosure complex at Durrington Walls, Wiltshire (Wainwright & Longworth 1971), which some regard as a ritual monument, particularly involving the slaughtering of and feasting on pigs and cattle, the latter often as bulls and steers (Richards & Thomas 1984). Deeper analysis of the prospects of ritual activity was based on the intrasite distribution of various pottery wares, flint artefacts and animal bones.

Colin Richards and Julian Thomas started by arguing that because the forms that cultures take frequently express the ways in which animals are categorised in a wide range of social concepts, then similar ideological differentiation was probably to be found in the spreads of bones at ancient sites. The evidence from artefacts allowed the checking '*of the hypothesis that different areas of Durrington Walls were treated differently for depositional purposes.*' (Richards & Thomas 1984). For reference a site plan is given Fig. 29. Chiefly the authors drew attention to percentage differences in the spreads of cattle and pig bones at Durrington Walls and attributed these differences to the conceptual worlds behind their prehistoric cultures.

Curiously, however, the action of other bone spread formation–processes like those in the model were scarcely

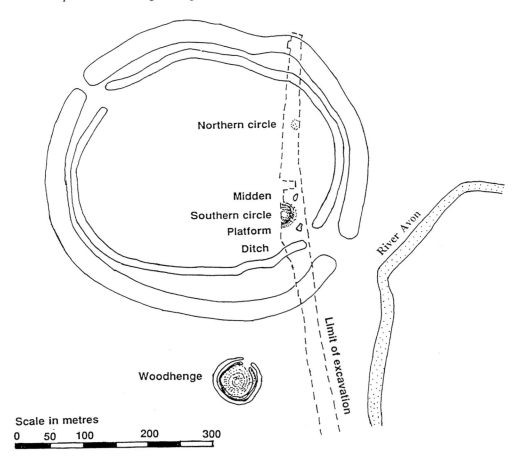

Fig. 29. Map of major structures and features at Durrington Walls (after several sources).

discussed. Yet it is here that the cross cultural model seems to clarify both the description and interpretation of the site bone debris, most obviously where bones in the Northern circle of postholes consisted entirely of those from cattle. First it should be noted that the bone group was a small sample and this may partly explain the absence of other species. Then, since it would label the cattle bones as coarse debris, the model indicates that the features of the Northern circle were peripheral to the main centres of bone–related site activity. Fig. 29 indicates that this area of the site was more remote from other major structures.

This reinterpretation is not necessarily inconsistent with the authors' suggestion that cattle butchery occurred in the Northern circle but, if they continued to argue this particular area was a special focus of ritual involving cattle, on the whole the paucity of bones recovered does not substantiate their contention. If ritual took place there, e.g. manipulation of pottery, it appears best explained as occurring independently of bone–related activities which appear more probably to have scattered bones there from other sources.

Much of the other bone debris excavated at Durrington Walls occurred close to the southwestern entrance to the monument and was comprised of more comparable mixtures of coarse and medium sized bones of cattle and pig. Greater prominence of cattle in the deposits of the Platform and the Old land surface indicate somewhat less intensive activity areas, while the bones from the Midden, Southern circle and the nearby enclosure Ditch had the greatest abundance of pig

among them and indicate the main areas of central and intense activity in the vicinity.

Going as far to designate the detritus as domestic debris as the cross cultural model generally would do is not particularly satisfactory for a Neolithic monumental site but the posing of this option does have the merit of querying the interpretation of the deposits as ritually special or structured ones. Thus the previous view of Geoffrey Wainwright of one of the deposits as a midden need not be so far wrong.

In pursuing the views of the authors, analysis of body parts was claimed to be meaningful but, as they noted, large numbers of loose teeth were prominent in the samples and therefore do not inspire confidence where included in the statistical analysis of elemental remains to investigate butchery. Nonetheless there appears to be a case made by inspection of the figures for specific elements in the superabundance of the back–limb bones of pig from the Midden, and of numerous vertebrae of pig from the Southern circle and from the Ditch. Little patterning is obvious among the skeletal element data of cattle bones as our modelling of bone dispersal would predict.

Where element data was summed into primary, secondary and waste bone groups, the pattern was admitted to be complicated; if anything it suggests to me that the butchery carried out was peculiar to each species. Yet, before other interpretations can be drawn, there is a main objection to the methods of the authors, and this is that the butchery model applied in the three part analysis is reminiscent of the medieval to modern 'economic pattern' of butchery. As described in Chapters 6 and 11, Iron Age and rural Romano–British butchery patterns, and possibly Neolithic ones are different to the medieval to modern urban patterning. Thus the butchery analysis of the authors is suspect.

A further point is that it appears reasonable to suggest that butchery was quick and did not exhaust the available nutritional content of bones so that the remains still may be indicative of feasting rather than of subsistence consumption. However, it is worth observing that amounts of waste from carcasses would also depend on how effective Neolithic people were at rearing animals for food and how generous or intimidated they were in supplying them to feed gatherings at monuments like Durrington Walls.

So, despite my evaluation of the ideas of Richards and Thomas, and the indications that most bone debris was ordinary in its associations, the suggestion that feasting occurred at the monument can not be rejected automatically. Eating of pork was certainly characteristic of this domestic/feasting activity but the model suggests that, less visibly, beef also was contributed to the activities involving pork consumption. Also to be remarked is that greater quantities of beef would have been obtained per bone of cattle than pork per bone of pig.

Where our thoughts turn to the presence of other species, the arguments of the authors for the intentional placement of wild and tame species bones appear largely speculative. The presence of large bones of wild boar and aurochs in the Ditch might simply be typical of this type of feature and its potentially mundane location rather than an indication of human conceptual schemes, coarse debris tending to predominate in relatively peripheral features although this part of the Ditch was close to one entrance and apparently close to a centre of site activity. Presence of uncommon species like horse or deer among the bones of the Southern circle may well be a function of the large sample size rather than to anything symbolically special about the deposition or the asociated former structures. It is conceded, however, that the incidence and pattern of deer remains at Maumbury Rings, Dorset (Bradley 1975), appears to have been significant through the eyes of the Neolithic participants.

Spacing of debris in the Southern circle at Durrington Walls was more closely explored. Typically, the spread of flints and Grooved ware tended to occur toward the peripheral rings of the concentric post holes (Richards & Thomas 1984, Fig.12.6). This suggests, although not investigated, that the bone debris, especially that of pig, would show a similar though more diffuse patterning. Thus the focus of the stone and bone related activities, e.g. eating, detritus clearance or butchery, might have occurred outside or on the periphery of the structure.

This predicted pattern can be contrasted with the distribution of bones at the adjacent Neolithic site of Woodhenge, Fig. 29, where pig debris was relatively abundant at the centre of the concentric ringed structure and cattle debris was more common toward the periphery (Thomas 1991, Fig. 4.6). Here, according to the model, intense activities appear focussed at the centre of the structure but there is too little information to decide to what extent symbolically directed schemes or ritual behaviour was involved.

Another site discussed in the structuring of bone deposits argued by Richards and Thomas is Neolithic and Beaker period Mount Pleasant, Dorset (Wainwright 1971). Pig bones predominated in the outer and palisade ditch groups while cattle bones predominated elsewhere, especially at Site IV, the internal timber circle. Again, interpretation using the model suggests it is not necessarily correct to envisage cattle being slaughtered at Site IV, whether or not it was a ritual enclosure; the sample size numbers are not particularly high and other general site processes like scavenging may explain the bones there. Greater activity however, especially meat eating, appears focussed in the vicinity of the outer and palisade ditches, perhaps between them and outside the 'ritual enclosure'. Thus greater and lesser sacred areas could have defined this monument.

Has the associated deposition of different types of pottery with the bones other explanations than the one of intentional deposition given by the authors? I only note here that at Durrington Walls the pottery type distribution with the greatest differences to other pot groups occurred in the Northern circle where the sample of bones was small and, as for the bones, a similar explanation of some potsherd ratios elsewhere is possible.

Elsewhere there is the discussion of I. J. Thorpe (1984, 51), apparently based on the observations of Leslie Grinsell (1958, 11 and 25–26), that the animal bones found at Neolithic long barrows tend to consist of cattle remains. This is interpreted or is implied to be an indication of ritual action or symbolism at the barrows and a reflection of the value and status of cattle in Neolithic culture. This may be so where cattle heads are prominent in features but on the whole there seems a shortage of information about these particular bone spreads. Alternatively modelled, the occurrences of cattle bones could be a result of nonritual bone related activities some distance away producing typical debris of consumption but spreading (by detritus clearance and scavenging) the coarser component as far as the ritual long barrow ditches and farther.

For example, the long or oval barrow excavated at Abingdon lay some 50 m from the causewayed enclosure there although it is not possible to properly confirm the deduction from the model since only two bones, interestingly both of cattle, were securely stratified in the barrow ditches (Levitan 1992, 138).

Thus although unfortunately we do not have as good documentation and analysis of Neolithic bone spreads as for spreads of later cultures, it can be seen readily that the present Neolithic depositional evidence and the current concensus of its explanations is still open to reinterpretation, albeit of more banal explication than the symbolic conceptions, structure and intentionality attributed to it. Some cases of intentional depositional symbolism involving deer antler or cattle skulls, however, may survive my revaluation of the evidence, as already indicated at Maumbury Rings and at other sites, such as at Barton Court Farm where one of three Neolithic pits contained a large antler and utilised cattle ribs amongst other bones (Miles 1986, Fiche 3A4–3B10 and 8A1–8C8).

Regretfully, at the general level of interpreting species remains, it is difficult to see how the assumptions of Richards, Thomas and others can be verified without more precise Neolithic spatial records and systematic analysis. Moreover, by largely ignoring the taphonomy of bone deposition (some aspects of butchery were discussed), these authors left their ideas open to criticism.

–0–

As a postscript, it is possible to relate similar modelling logic to spreads of site debris deposited during the Palaeolithic and Plio–Pleistocene periods. One may go as far back as the accurately mapped hominid occupation floors of the Olduvai Gorge, Tanzania. Patches of coarse bone debris and relatively fewer stone artefacts are evident by inspection amongst the commoner relatively homogeneous distribution of smaller debris (Leakey 1971, Figs. 24, 32, 35 and 47). Obviously, the study of such material is for expert specialists with an excellent knowledge of the taphonomy of such spreads (Potts 1988 and Ringrose 1993), but the field is an exciting one where the origin and the nature of humanity is pondered and debated. Tempted thus, some discussion of the applicability of the bone spacing model to the patterning of the occupation floors may be useful.

Following my belated and cursory observation of the spread of debris at Olduvai, it was found that an exacting analysis of it was made years before. Milla Ohel (1977) perceived there were circular concentrations of smaller bone debris and stone debitage which were significantly different to other debris of less dense distribution and greater size which formed elongate spreads, sometimes alongside the circular spreads. Stone tool distributions displayed little patterning. Elongate spreads were suggested to be places of butchery while circular concentrations were suggested to be eating and rubbish dropping areas. This interpretation is similar to the reasoning of the spatial model for post–Palaeolithic sites if circular concentrations were regarded as central areas of hominid activity while elongate concentrations could be regarded as peripheral ones.

Since the analysis of Ohel, the assumption that Olduvai hominids lived by hunting has been challenged. Binford and others (Binford 1985, and Binford, Mills & Stone 1986) have argued that many of the excavated bones were obtained by hominid scavenging from kills of other animal predators. Therefore the spreads of coarse debris can hardly be regarded as butchering places of whole carcasses in the way one attributes to later occupation spreads of pastoralists and other life–mode peoples. While some butchery of scavenged bones and meat, such as limb joint disarticulation, may have occurred in the elongate areas, other explanations of the coarse debris there seem required.

Storage of scavenged bones in the elongate peripheral areas is possible and perhaps some larger unutilised bones and fragments were trampled into the fine grained sediments thereby giving the observed effect. Alternatively, secondary scavenging might have destroyed many bones and scattered surviving large bones from the main accumulations in the circular areas. To this latter possibility, the central areas do appear created through specific actions such as the crushing of bones for marrow and the discard or abandonment of the smaller fragments. It is conceivable also that the spreads of large bones resulted from detritus clearance from the central circular areas.

Of all these explanations, the suggestion that hominids kept the implied central and food consumption areas fairly free of coarse rubbish would be the most controversial yet it may be a viable explanation. Detritus clearance might be regarded as a human trait but it is conceivable that a hominid species in transition to man might display this behaviour.

If this suggestion appears too radical, one could be guided by the cautious views of Richard Potts (1988, 247–311) and let others evaluate our model in a detailed analysis of hominid spreads of bones. In this, one could discuss the provocative question of whether a symbolic or ritual explanation of hominid bone debris, as might be implicit by the work of Hodder and others, can be accepted or rejected.

Chapter 17

Complexity of Modelling and Giving Ritual its Place

Books come to an end but most narrative continues tangibly. New books appear, transforming syncretic monologue into dialogue. Critics of the text in production and book reviewers bring fresh points to bear in the restless mind. This last chapter is a synthesis of intellectual influences during 1993 and an elaboration of the previous chapters of discussion.

First point to be made is to emphasise the need to develop and improve excavation techniques and mapping precision in the confirmation or denial of the spatial and other patterns of bones and artefacts at a variety of future sites. Excavation directors examining prospective sites must select ones that are suitable to reveal patterning and allow both time and work to adequately test supposition and questions arising from this book. Especially, sieving controls on recovery of different types of debris must be improved and be adequate to the task. Coherent well–differentiated and well–preserved settlements and their peripheral areas must be chosen and substantially and systematicly excavated, with recording of bones and artefacts at least to the nearest metre of a site grid system. Small and unsystematic excavations of settlements, poorly preserved and incoherently structured sites appear unsuitable for this research.

Second, it appears necessary to stress the complexity of factors involved in the overall taphonomy of bone deposition (Payne pers. comm.). Although the model in this book lists and discusses at least three main processes involved in the spatial patterning of bones, other factors are implicated. Recently attention has been directed again to the effects of trampling on bones in a study by Rebecca Nicholson (1992). While it is not clear what quantitative impact trampling had on the differential destruction of all types of bone debris, it appears probable now that trampling was a significant part in the destruction of smallest bones like those of fish in external areas such as in the yards of the manor house at Hardings Field. Fish bones were virtually absent among the sieved bones from a peripheral area, possibly the vineyard, of Abingdon Abbey (Wilson unpub. j). My model predicts they should rarely be there but it is also possible that trampling reduced any of them to unrecovered powder.

Further investigation also appears necessary in the characterisation of floor, 'occupation', demolition, and post–destruction deposits. In one paper, K. Mathews (1992) discusses deposits at a Saxon and medieval settlement at Letchworth, Hertfordshire. Not having observed much of the excavations at Hardings Field, little can be said further on the designation there of floor, occupation and dumping levels but I and others have excavated Roman floors and dumping levels at Twickenham House, Abingdon (Wilson & Wallis 1991), and limited results there do parallel descriptions and bone patterns at Hardings Field. From Philip Page's description of the deposits in Room A9 at the manor house as possessing a concave cross section, it would not be surprising if the floor of this room had finally served as a

chicken run or pigsty into which table refuse from elsewhere was dumped as animal food but this is speculation. All that can be concluded really is that the nature of the bone refuse and its spatial context fits general expectations of the taphonomic processes in a predominately earthen floored house and, importantly, throughout two or three phases of occupation.

Here again it is worth returning to the apparent strength of the association of medium coarse debris with houses and hearths at Mingies Ditch. Broadly speaking, this conclusion is acceptable but the cpmplexity of stratigraphy and individual bone spreads is greater than that implied by the method of lumping together of all bones from deposits, including those from possible destruction and midden deposits of adjoining houses being spread over the surroundings of any one house under consideration.

–0–

Ironically, the more precise we become about the spatial patterning of bones at individual sites, we may gain little more accuracy in the quantitative contributions of each of the formation processes involved in accumulating and distributing bones. Cultural factors are particularly difficult to quantify. This issue becomes even more acute when we try to examine the impact of ritual on the deposition of bones. The modelling so far has not accomodated ritual and symbolic action well in the largely functional interpretations of bone debris.

To an extent, ritual has been a taphonomic afterthought. This is not due to its lack of interest but because usually it is very difficult to recognise the effects of ritual action in deposits and because the definition and nature of ritual has been a matter of no little debate in archaeology and anthropology.

Toward resolving the problematic issue of ritual, however, Catherine Bell (1992) has comprehensively reviewed the anthropological literature and has provided a synthesis assisting thought in this field. Some outcomes of her work are:–

> '.... several features emerge as very common to ritualization: strategies of differentiation through formalization and periodicity, the centrality of the body, the orchestrations of schemes by which the body defines an environment and is defined in turn by it, ritual mastery, and the negotiation of power to appropriate and define the hegemonic order.' (Bell 1992, 220).

> '.... the type of authority formulated by ritualization tends to make ritual activities effective in grounding and displaying a sense of community without overriding the autonomy of individuals or subgroups.' (1992, 221–22).

Bell is clearly concerned with the psychology of the individual and the community, a theme which may be exemplified by a brief excursion on the nature of place and space in ritual as dealt with by Jonathan Smith (1992). In his rejection of the abstract spatial interpretation of Mircea Eliade of Tjilapa (Australian) and other cultural myths, great emphasis is put on the notion of place as a focus of value, meaning and concrete experience. Place, meaning and experience, however, become increasingly elaborate and abstract in middle eastern cultures, especially in the layout and ritual use of temples. Moreover, with the territorial loss of Jerusalem from Judaism and, especially Christianity, the concreteness and accessibility of place was lost from religious thought and action, even to pilgrimage. What remained was a cultural narrative and a commendation to translocate religious meaning into inner spatial schemes.

The careful and detailed exegesis of Smith can not be elaborated here but it seems that the end of his text and that of Bell has come full circle in examining ritual place and space and opens up a wide range of possibilities for understanding ritual phenomena. But as psychology it is remote from its application in archaeology. Neither do we yet possess an adequate definition of ritual, nor has ritual been satisfactorily distinguished from other behaviour except that ritual appears largely to focuss on the inner workings of religious activity.

It is as the outer manifestations of religion that archaeology has approached ritual, for example the work of Wait (1985), Garwood and others (1991) while Merrifield (1987) has devoted text also to superstitions. In the absence of amplification about the nature of ritual and a definitive categorisation of social and cultural processes which relate bones in place and space, it appears possible only to adopt and apply a hybrid monster of unreconciled philosophical methodology to examine the classification of bone remains and their significance.

Table 20 schematises relationships between explanatory paradigms, settlement activities, and context types of bone detritus where these classes can be, or have been so far, differentiated. There is no pretence that the scheme is a complete and unflawed characterisation of the cultural forms and contexts of human activities. It does attempt to show, however, the wide range of activities and types of bone detritus which can be grouped under both ceremonial and domestic activity spheres, and under the ideas of informal meal consumption, feasting and sacrificial spheres. In short it is intended to show a scheme of ritual, ritualized and non ritual categories.

Although even domestic activity is not immune to some ritualization, e.g. the saying of grace at meals, at least some domestic activity can be distinguished from intense ritual and therefore domestic and profane or mundane places can be distinguished in theory from sacred places. To assist this recognition, it seems useful in the table to separate between ordinary butchery and that undertaken as a part of the making of sacrifices.

It has appeared worth adding another class of place, that of places 'other than' of the classes mentioned as a specific part of normal domestic activity areas, such as domestic rooms, or of specific sacrificial places such as shrines and temples. Thus, for example, it is possible to include Iron Age storage pits, argued by some to be part of sacrificial or propitiatory rituals (Grant 1984 and 1989 and Cunliffe 1992), as well as manor halls where high status banquets were held.

The lower half of the table concerns the type of bone detritus which may identify the occurrence of specific former activities in the places listed above. Four levels of identification appear possible.

First, where there is proper evidence of past formally or symbolically structured situations. This includes the religious positioning of bones in specific places like shrines, as well as high status activities like feasting or hunting which leave either distinctive species bones behind or with evidence of bones being displayed in prominent places, such as (Sadler 1990) fallow antlers having been nailed to walls.

Second, there are bone deposits which are only evidence of informally structured situations. Thus it seems possible to recognise ordinary table refuse, at least that which shows no tangible evidence of ritualization like banqueting. Another example of informally structured deposits would be butchery waste from trades and industries. Also in theory at least, there are remains informally discarded during or after formally structured rituals using some carcass parts but not others.

Third, there is bone debris which is sufficiently damaged and disordered to obscure most evidence of the cultural events that it was part of. While most cultural information would be lost due to processes like scavenging and trampling, there might be sufficient representation of unusual species remaining to indicate something of its cultural circumstances. Classified at this level of identification is the abundance of goat bones, especially of males, in parts of the shrine assemblage at Uley Hill, Gloucestershire (chapter 15).

As an example of the usefulness of these distinctions, and in the absence of evidence to the contrary as yet, the 'intentionally deposited and structured' bone debris discussed for Durrington Walls by Richards and Thomas (chapter 16) appears to fall into the second or third levels of identification rather than into the first to which its misleading labelling might at first appear to classify it.

Fourth, there is bone debris which is so degraded and uniformative, even in the light of excavation contexts and spatial patterning, little can be said confidently about its involvement in the cultural past.

These four levels of identification or interpretation of bone debris appear usefully differentiated in the table since it becomes clear that the data from bones sometimes will fall into more than one place and more than one level of interpretation. This means that on bone information alone it may be difficult and even impossible to distinguish the true nature of bones which have been uncovered. Thus the ambiguous significance of some bone deposits demonstrated here are more examples of equifinality: the principle that different mechanisms or processes may produce the same type of artefactual or ecofactual detritus.

Sometimes, of course, contextual analysis beyond the spatial location above, e.g. using architectual and historial information, may clarify the significance of the bones. The importance of contextual explanation has been especially emphasised by Hodder.

It is hoped that, crude though it is, the scheme of Table 20 will promote the understanding of cultural complexity while making clear the limitations of bone evidence. While many assemblages will never reveal the true intricacy of past cultural matters and their cognitive phenomena, at least we are able of revising our attitudes as we resolve problems of interpretation. In particular, we may increase our mental dexterity about what constitutes the economies of other cultures while allowing for the diversity of their values, symbolism and behaviour (Garwood et al 1991, v–viii).

To discuss the definition of economy takes us beyond the book brief of demonstrating and explaining spatial patterning but it is recognised here that the symbolic systems of cultures influence and substantially modify what can be understood to be basic models of economic and ergonomic thinking and not just of an economy of Western cultural form. For this reason the spatial and processual model proposed in this book has to be envisaged, in some cases, as being modified by the conceptual and value structures of certain cultures it may be applied to. An instance is the behaviour of the Samburu (Pavitt 1991), a semi–nomadic pastoralist people in Kenya evidently practising butchery in ritual circumstances beyond the fixity of settlements like that presumed to exist at Mingies Ditch. But substantial work on this and other archaeological issues appears required before that book can be written.

Table 20 Identifying interpretive relationships between site activities and bone evidence

	Functional/systemic/processual				Ritual/post-processual	
Explanatory paradigm						
General sphere of activity	Domestic activity				Ceremonial activity	
	Trade/industry					
Spatial context	Butchery place.	Cooking place.	Eating place.	Other place.	Materially distinct religious place/space.	Wider demarcated ritual space and place
Examples	Yard, slaughter house.	Exposed hearth, kitchen.	Open area, dining room.	Pit/shaft, palace, hall.	Temple, shrine or cemetery.	Slaughtering place: inside/outside
Further definitive activity zones			Meal consumption		Sacrificial offering	
				Feasting		
Nature of bones.						
1. Evidence of formally or symbolically structured situation	Absent, although functional butchery can be represented symbolically				Specific items such as articulated limb, skulls and whole skeletons, formally placed	
2. Informally structured evidence	Butchery and industrial refuse including articulated bones from large species and high percentages of specific elements from others		Table refuse of special communal or high status meals including unusual or prestigious animal species or ritual display items, eg. heads and articulated remains of small species		Table refuse, especially medium fine debris, certain skeletal elements and articulated bones of smaller species	
3. Disordered bone debris	Skeletal elements		Skeletons from non ritual burial of diseased or worn out animals		Similar or different species present	Similar or different species present
4. Degraded or insufficient bone debris lacking structural/social context obscured by other taphonomic processes.						

EPILOGUE

During and after the mid 1970's there has been a flow of publications at least partly connected with the spatial patterning of bones and sometimes pottery on settlement sites. Yet intrasite spatial analysis has been of lesser importance in the minds of archaeologists, probably because significant spatial patterning among bones appears only recognised consistently in the cross cultural work on sites in the Upper Thames Valley. Even this has been published slowly and little evaluated further. That there is a pattern among coarse and fine debris recovered at a wider number of sites appears hardly disputable but it is necessary for others to look for convincing similar trends elsewhere.

Conceivably, but doubtfully, such patterning is a product of sampling and recovery techniques; systemmatic sieving of central and peripheral areas of site spreads has yet to demonstrate whether significant differential recovery of bones was likely to have been involved in the results obtained in the Upper Thames Valley. On the other hand, early in the investigation of bone patterning, an explanatory model was proposed and predicted trends like those observed (although this does not negate the point about possible differential bone recovery). Moreover, the proposed model invokes general site processes which explain the spread of bones at sites of different periods, such as Mingies Ditch and Hardings Field.

Both relatively simple and more complex variation in settlement and feature patterning are evident. The problem now is that it may be too difficult to quantify the input of each contributory process, especially where general processes like rubbish clearance are constituted of any of a variety of particular and even unique actions, such as bone dropping, kicking and throwing aside. We can not usually identify much of the specific causality of an isolated bone but, where sizeable and coherent excavations are undertaken and spatial patterns are recognised, we can generate in our minds a good general understanding of the causality of that patterning and of individual bones within that patterning. From such occurrences and parallel and complete analyses on a multitude of sites, we glean a contribution to what was happening in the immediate and the wider ecology and culture of each settlement.

REFERENCES AND BIBLIOGRAPHY

Allen K. M. S., Green S. W. & Zubrow E. B. W. 1990, *Interpreting space: GIS and archaeology*, London: Taylor and Francis.

Allen T. G. 1981, 'Hardwick–with–Yelford; Smiths Field', *CBA–9 Newsletter* 11, 124–27.

– 1990, *An Iron Age and Romano–British enclosed settlement at Watkins Farm, Northmoor, Oxon.*, Thames Valley Landscapes: the Windrush Valley 1.

Allen T. G. & Robinson M. 1979, 'Hardwick–with–Yelford', *CBA–9 Newsletter* 9, 115–17.

– 1993, *The prehistoric landscape and Iron Age enclosed settlement at Mingies Ditch, Hardwick–with–Yelford, Oxon.*, Thames Valley Landscapes: the Windrush Valley 2.

Ammerman A. J., Gifford D. P. & Voorrips A. 1978, 'Toward an evaluation of sampling strategies', in *Simulation studies in archaeology*, ed. I. Hodder, Cambridge: Cambridge University Press, 123–36, Fig. 1.

Ardener S. (ed) 1993, *Women and space: ground rules and social maps* (2nd edn), Providence, USA: Berg Publishers Ltd.

Armitage P. L. 1984, 'Preliminary report on the cattle horn cores from Greyfriars', in Hassall T., Halpin C. E. & Mellor M., Excavations in St Ebbe's, Oxford, 1967–76: part II, *Oxoniensia* xlix, fiche MVI B2.

– 1989, 'The use of animal bones as building material in post–medieval Britain', and 'Gazateer of sites with animal bones used as building material', in Serjeantson & Waldron below, 147–60 and 201–23.

Avery M. 1982, 'The Neolithic causewayed enclosure', Abingdon in Case and Whittle below, 10–50.

Barker G. 1978, 'Economic models for the Manekweni Zimbabwe, Mozambique', *Azania* XIII, 71–100.

Barker G. & Webley D. 1978, 'Causewayed camps and Neolithic economies', *Proceedings of the Prehistoric society* 44, 161–186.

Bartram, L.E., Kroll E. M. & Bunn H. T. 1991, 'Variability in camp structure and bone food refuse patterning at Kua San hunter–gatherer camps, in Kroll & Price below, 77–148.

Bell C. 1992, *Ritual theory, ritual practice*, New York: Oxford University Press.

Binford L. R. (ed.) 1977, *For theory building in archaeology*, New York: Academic Press.

– 1978a, Dimensional analysis of behavior and site structure: learning from an Eskimo hunting stand, *American Antiquity* 43 (3), 330–361.

– 1978b, *Nunamiut ethnoarchaeology*, New York: Academic Press.

– 1981, *Bones: ancient men and modern myths*, New York: Academic Press.

– 1983, *In Pursuit of the past*, Thames and Hudson.

– 1985, 'Human ancestors: changing views of their behavior', reprinted in Binford 1989 below, 301–28.

– 1987, 'Researching ambiguity: frames of reference and structure', reprinted in Binford 1989 below, 223–63.

– 1989, *Debating archaeology*, San Diego: Academic Press.

Binford L. R. & Bertram J. B. 1977, 'Bone frequencies and attritional processes', in Binford 1977 above, 77–153.

Binford L. R., Mills M. G. L. & Stone N. M. 1988, 'Hyaena scavenging behavior and its implications for the interpretation of faunal assemblages from FLK22 (the Zinj floor) at Olduvai Gorge', reprinted in Binford 1989 above, 352–82.

Blair J. & Ramsay N. 1991, *English medieval industries*, London: Hambledon Press.

Blankholm H. P. 1991, *Intrasite analysis in theory and practice*, Aarhus: Aarhus University Press.

Bradley R. 1975, 'Maumbury Rings, Dorchester: the excavations of 1908–1913', *Archaeologia* 105, 1–97.

– 1986, 'A reinterpretation of the Abingdon causewayed enclosure', *Oxoniensia* li, 183–87.

– 1992, The excavation of an oval barrow beside the Abingdon causewayed enclosure, Oxfordshire', *Proceedings of the Prehistoric society* 58, 127–42.

Bradley R. & Fulford M. 1980, 'Sherd size in the analysis of occupation debris', *Bulletin of the Institute of Archaeology* 17, 85–94.

Bradley R. & Gardiner J. (eds.) 1984, *Neolithic studies: a view of some current research*, British Archaeological Report (British series) 133.

Brain C. K. 1967, Hottentot food remains and their bearing on the interpretation of fossil bone assemblages, *Scientific Papers of the Namib Desert Research Station* 32, 1–11.

– 1976, 'Some principles in the interpretation of bone accumulations associated with man', in *Human origins: Louis Leakey and the East African evidence*, ed. G. L. Isaac & H. R. McCown, Berkley: Staples Press, 97–116.

Briggs G., Cook J. & Rowley T. (eds.) 1986, *The archaeology of the Oxford Region, Oxford*, Oxford University Department for External Studies.

Britnall W. 1989, 'The Collfryn hillslope enclosure, Llansant Denddwr, Powys: Excavations 1980–1982', *Papers of the Prehistoric Society* 55, 89–134.

Brodribb A. C. C., Hands A. R. & Walker D. R. 1968–1978, *Excavations at Shakenoak Farm, near Wilcote, Oxfordshire*, British Archaeological Reports I–V.

Bulmer R. 1976, 'Selectivity in hunting and in disposal of animal bone by the Kalam of the New Guinea highlands', in *Problems of economic archaeology*, ed. G. de G. Sieveking, I. H. Longworth & K. E. Wilson, London: Duckworth, 169–86.

Carr C. 1984, 'The nature of intrasite archaeological records and spatial analytical processes and their investigation', in *Advances in Archaeological Method*, ed. M. B. Schiffer 7, 103–222.

– 1985 (1989), *For concordance in archaeological analysis*, Illinois: Waveland Press, 297–500.

– 1991, Left in the dust: contextual information in model–focussed archaeology, in Kroll & Price below, 257–68.

Case H. 1956, 'The Neolithic causewayed camp at

Abingdon, Berks.', *Antiquaries Journal* 36 11–30.

Case H. & Whittle A. W. R. 1982, *Settlement patterns in the Oxford region: excavations at the Abingdon causewayed enclosure and other sites*, Council of British Archaeology Research Report 44.

Chambers R. 1978, 'Chalgrove, Hardings Field, moated site', *CBA–9 Newsletter* 8, 110–12.

Chaplin R. E. 1971, *The study of animal bones from archaeological sites*, London: Seminar Press.

Cherry J. 1991, 'Leather', in Blair & Ramsay above, 295–318.

Cherry J., Gamble C. & Shennan S. 1978, *Sampling in contemporary British archaeology*, British Archaeological Reports (British series) 50.

Clarke D. 1977, 'Spatial information in archaeology', in *Spatial archaeology*, ed. D. Clarke, London: Academic Press, 1–32.

Coy J. 1981, in C. Gingell, 'Excavation of an Iron Age settlement at Groundwell Farm, Blunsdon St Andrew 1976', *Wiltshire Archaeological and Natural History Magazine* 76, 68–74.

– 1987, in P. J. Fasham, 'A banjo enclosure in Micheldever Wood, Hampshire', *Hampshire Field Club Monograph* 5, 45–48.

Cram L. et al. 1968–1978, Bone reports in Brodribb et al. above.

– 1982, in Avery & Whittle above, 43–46.

Cribb R. 1991, *Nomads in archaeology*, Cambridge: Cambridge University Press.

Cunliffe B. 1983, *Danebury: anatomy of an Iron Age hillfort*, London: Batsford, 155–71.

– 1992, 'Pits, preoccupations and propitiation in the British Iron Age', *Oxford Journal of Archaeology* 11 (1), 69–83.

Davis S. 1986, *Animals in archaeology*, London: Batsford.

Durham B. in prep., *Oxford before the university*, Thames Valley Landscapes Monograph.

Edwards E. H. 1987, *Horses: their role in the history of man*, London: BBC publications.

Eisenstadt S. N. 1967, 'Social change, differentiation and evolution', in *System, change and conflict*, ed. N. J. Demerath III & R. A. Peterson, New York: Free Press, 213–29.

Ellison A. 1981, 'Natives, Romans and Christians on West Hill, Uley', in *Roman Britain*, ed. W. Rodwell, British Archaeological Report (British series) 77, 305–20.

Fasham P. 1985, 'The prehistoric settlement at Winnall Down, Winchester', *Hampshire Field Club Monograph* 2.

Ferring C. R. 1984, 'Intrasite spatial patterning: its role in settlement subsistence systems analysis', in Hietala 1984a below, 116–25.

Fieller F. C., Gilbertson D.D. & Ralph N.G. (eds.) 1985, *Palaeobiological investigations*, British Archaeological Reports (International series) 266.

Fotheringham S. & Rogerson P. 1994, *Spatial analysis and GIS*, London: Taylor and Francis.

Frazer F.C. 1956, in Case H., 'The Neolithic causewayed camp at Abingdon, Berks.', *Antiquaries Journal* xxxvi, 11–30.

Gamble C. 1978, 'Optimising information from studies of faunal remains', in Cherry et al. above, 321–54.

Garwood P., Jennings D., Skeats R. & Toms J. 1991, Sacred and profane, *Oxford University Committee for Archaeology Monograph* 32.

Gifford D.P. 1980, 'Ethnological observations of natural processes affecting cultural materials', in Gould below, 77–101.

Gifford D.P. & Behrensmeyer A. 1977, 'Observed formation and burial of a recent occupation site in Kenya', *Quaternary Research* 8 (2), 245–66.

Gifford–Gonzalez D. P., Damrosch D. B., Damrosch D. R., Pryor J. & Thunen R. L. 1985, 'The third dimension in site structure: an experiment in trampling and vertical dispersal', *American Antiquity*, 50 (4), 803–18.

Gould R. 1980, *Explorations in ethnoarchaeology*, Albuqueque: University of New Mexico Press.

Grant A. 1978, 'Animal bones', in Bradley R., Rescue excavations in Dorchester–on–Thames, *Oxoniensia* xliii, 40–47.

– 1980, in Rowley T. & Brown L., 'Excavations at Beach House Hotel, Dorchester–on–Thames, *Oxoniensia* xlvi, 1–55.

– 1984, in *Danebury: an Iron Age hillfort in Hampshire*, ed. B. Cunliffe, Council of British Archaeology Research Report 52 (2), 486–547.

– 1989, Animals in early Britain: the visible and the invisible, *Anthropozoologica* 3, 79–86.

Grinsell L. V. 1958, *The archaeology of Wessex*, London: Methuen.

Halpin C. E., 1983, 'Late Saxon evidence and excavation of Hinxey Hall,

Queen Street, Oxford', *Oxoniensia* xlviii, 41–65.

Halstead P., Hodder I. & Jones G. 1978, 'Behavioural archaeology and refuse patterns', *Norwegian Archaeological Review* 11 (2), 118–31.

Harcourt R. 1986, in Musty J. & Algar D., 'Excavations at the DMV of Gomeldon, Salisbury', *Wiltshire Archaeological and Natural History Magazine* 80, 166–69.

Harman M. 1981, in Williams J. H. & Shaw M., St Peters, Northampton, 328–332.

Harman M. 1985, in Lambrick below, 190–93.

Harvey P. D. A. 1965, *A medieval Oxfordshire village: Cuxham 1240–1400*, Oxford: University Press.

Hassall T. 1986, *Archaeology of Oxford city*, in Briggs et al. above, 115–134.

– 1987, *Oxford: the buried city*, Oxford: Oxfordshire Archaeological Unit.

Hassall T., Halpin C. E. & Mellor M. 1984, 'Excavations in St Ebbe's, Oxford, Part II: post–medieval domestic tenements and the post–dissolution site of the Greyfriars, *Oxoniensia* xlix, 153–275.

– 1989, 'Excavations in St Ebbe's, Oxford, 1967–1976, Part I: late Saxon and medieval domestic occupation and tenements and the medieval Greyfriars, *Oxoniensia* liv, 71–277.

Hesse B. & Wapnish P. 1985, *Animal bone archeology: from objectives to analysis*, Washington: Taraxacum.

Hietala H. J. (ed.) 1984a, *Intrasite spatial analysis in*

archaeology, Cambridge: University Press.

– 1984b, 'Intrasite spatial analysis: a brief review', in Hietala above, 1–3.

Hill J. D. 1995, *Ritual and Rubbish in the Iron Age of Wessex*, British Archaeological Reports (British series) 242.

Hinchliffe J. & Thomas R. 1980, 'Archaeological investigations at Appleford', *Oxoniensia* xlv, 9–111.

Hingley R. & Miles D. 1984, 'Aspects of Iron Age settlement in the Upper Thames Valley', in *Aspects of the Iron Age in central southern Britain*, ed. B. Cunliffe & D. Miles, University of Oxford Committee for Archaeology Monograph 2, 52–71.

Hivernal F. & Hodder I. 1984, 'Analysis of artifact distributions at Ngenya (Kenya): depositional and post–depositional effects', in Hietala 1984a above, 97–115.

Hodder I. 1978, *The spatial organisation of culture*, London: Duckworth.

– 1982a, *Symbols in action*, Cambridge: University Press.

– 1982b, *Symbolic and structural archaeology*, Cambridge: University Press.

– 1985a, 'Postprocessual archaeology', in *Advances in Archaeological Method and Theory* 8, 1–25.

– 1985b, *Reading the past*, Cambridge: University Press.

– 1989, 'Postmodernism, poststructuralism and postprocessual archaeology', in *The meaning of things: material culture and symbolic expression*, ed. I Hodder, London: Unwin and Hyman, 64–78.

– 1992, *Theory and practice in archaeology*, London: Routledge.

Hodder I. & Orton C. 1976, *Spatial analysis in archaeology*, Cambridge: University Press.

Hofman J. L. & Enloe J. E. 1992, *Piecing together the past: applications of refitting studies in archaeology*, British Archaeological Report (International Series) 578.

Holmes, J. 1993, in R. J. Williams, *Pennyland Hartigans: two Iron Age and Saxon sites in Milton Keynes*, Buckinghamshire Archaeological Society Monograph 4, 133–54.

Isaac G.L. 1967, 'Towards the interpretation of occupation debris: some experiments and observations', *Kroeber Anthropology Society Papers* 37, 31–55.

– 1971, The diet of early man, *World Archaeology* 2 (3), 280–83.

Johnson I. 1984, Cell frequency recording and analaysis of artifact distributions, in Hietala 1984a above, 75–96.

Jones M. 1978, Sampling in a rescue context, in Cherry et al. above, 191–206.

Jones R. T. unpublished, Ancient Monuments Laboratory Report 1952.

Kent S. (ed.) 1990, *Domestic architecture and the use of space*, Cambridge: University Press.

King A. C. 1978, 'A comparative study of bone assemblages from Roman sites in Britain', *Bulletin of the Institute of Archaeology, London* 15, 207–32.

Kroll E. M. & Isaac G. L. 1984, 'Spatial configurations of artifacts and bones at early Pleistocene sites in East Africa', in Hietala 1984a above, 4–31.

Kroll E. M. & Price D. T. (eds.) 1991, *The interpretation of archaeological spatial patterning*, New York: Plenum Press.

Lambrick G. 1978, 'Berinsfield, Mount Farm', *CBA–9 Newsletter* 8, 108–10.

– 1979, 'Berinsfield, Mount Farm', *CBA–9 Newsletter* 9, 113–15.

– 1985, 'Further excavations on the second site of the Dominican Priory, Oxford', *Oxoniensia* l, 131–208.

– unpublished a, Excavations at Mount Farm, Berinsfield, Oxon.

– unpublished b, Excavations at Gravelly Guy Stanton Harcourt, Oxon.

Lambrick G. & Robinson M. 1979, *Iron Age and Roman riverside settlements at Farmoor*, Oxon., Council of British Archaeology Research Report 32.

Leakey M. D. 1971, *Olduvai Gorge: excavations in Beds I and II 1960–63*, Cambridge: University Press.

Levitan B. 1989, Bone analysis and urban economy, in Serjeantson & Waldron below, 161–88.

– 1990a, in Saville A. *Hazelton North, Gloucestershire 1979–1982*, English Heritage Archaeological Report 13, 199–213.

– 1990b, in Bell M., *Brean Down excavations 1983–1987*, English Heritage Archaeological Report 15, 220–41.

– 1992, in Bradley above, 138.

– 1993, in Woodward & Leach below, 257–301.

Lloyd C. 1993, *Structures in history*, Oxford: Blackwell.

Locker A. 1987, in Neal D. S., 'Excavations at Magiovinium, Buckinghamshire 1978–80', *Records of Buckinghamshire* 29, 108–15.

Luff R. & Rowley–Conwy P. eds. 1994, *Whither environmental archaeology?*, Oxbow Monograph 38.

Lyman R. L. 1994, *Vertebrate taphonomy*, New York: Cambridge University Press.

MacGregor A. 1991, 'Antler, bone and horn', in Blair and Ramsay above, 355–78.

Malina J. & Vasicek Z. 1990, *Archaeology yesterday and today*, Cambridge: University Press, 60–66.

Maltby M. 1979, The animal bones from Exeter 1971–1975, *Exeter Archaeological Reports* 2, 13–21 and 38–40.

– 1981, 'Iron Age, Romano–British and Anglo–Saxon animal husbandry – a review of the evidence', in *The environment of man: the Iron Age to the Anglo–Saxon period*, ed. M. Jones & G. Dimbleby, British Archaeological Report 87, 155–203.

– 1982, 'The variability of faunal samples and their effects on ageing data', in Wilson, Grigson & Payne below, 81–90.

– 1985a, Report in Fasham above, 97–112.

– 1985b, 'Patterns in faunal assemblage variability', in *Beyond domestication in prehistoric Europe*, ed. G. Barker & C. Gamble, 49–74.

Martin A. F. & Steele R. W. 1954, *The Oxford Region*, Oxford: University Press.

Mathews K. 1993, 'A futile occupation?: archaeological meanings and archaeological deposits', in *Interpreting stratigraphy*, ed. J. W. Barber,

Edinburgh: AOC Scotland Ltd, 55–61.

Mathews W. & Postgate J. N. with Payne S., Charles M. P. & Dobney K. 1994, in Luff & Rowly–Conwy above, 171–242.

Meadow R. 1975, 'Mammmal remains from Hadji Firuz: a study in methodology', in *Archaeozoological studies*, ed. A. T. Clason, 265–283.

– 1991, *Harappa excavations 1986–90*, Monographs in World Archaeology 3, 97–103.

Merrifield R. 1987, *The archaeology of ritual and magic*, London: Batsford, 128–31.

Miles D. 1980, 'Lechlade/Fairford, Claydon Pike', *CBA–9 Newsletter* 10, 160–64.

– 1986, *Archaeology at Barton Court Farm, Abingdon, Oxon.*, Council of British Archaeology Research Report 50.

Miles D. & Palmer S. 1981, 'Fairford/Lechlade, Claydon Pike', *CBA–9 Newsletter* 11, 144–46.

– 1982, 'Fairford/Lechlade, Claydon Pike', *CBA–9 Newsletter* 12, 164–71.

– 1983, 'Fairford/Lechlade, Claydon Pike', *South Midlands Archaeology*, 108–11.

– in prep., *Excavations at Lechlade and Claydon Pike*, Gloucestershire.

Moore H. L. 1981, 'Bone refuse – possibilities for the future', in *Economic archaeology*, eds. G. Bailey & A. Sheridan, British Archaeological Reports (British series) 96, 87–94.

– 1982, 'The interpretation of spatial patterning in settlement residues', in Hodder 1982b above, 74–79.

Nicholson R. 1992, 'Bone survival: the effects of sedimentary abrasion and trampling on fresh and cooked bone', *International Journal of Osteoarchaeology* 2 (1), 79–90.

O'Connor T. P. 1986, 'The animal bones', in Zienkiewicz J. D., *The legionary fortress baths at Carleon, II The finds*, Cardiff: National Museum of Wales, 224–88.

– 1991, 'Science, evidential archaeology and the new scholasticism', *Scottish Archaeological Review* 8, 1–7.

Ohel M. 1977, 'Patterned concentrations on living floors at Olduvai, Beds I and II: experimental study', *Journal of Field Archaeology* 4, 423–33.

Page P. 1979, 'Chalgrove, Hardings Field', *CBA–9 Newsletter* 9, 118–23.

– 1980, 'Chalgrove, Hardings Field', *CBA–9 Newsletter* 10, 151–52.

– 1982, 'Chalgrove, Hardings Field', *CBA–9 Newsletter* 12, 172–75.

– 1983, 'Chalgrove, Hardings Field', *South Midlands Archaeology*, 117–20.

– et al. unpublished, *Excavations at Hardings Field, Chalgrove, Oxon.*

Parker Pearson M. & Richards C. (eds) 1994, *Architecture and order: approaches to social space*, London: Routledge.

Parrington M. 1978, *Excavation at an Iron Age settlement at Ashville Trading Estate, Abingdon, Oxon.*, Council of British Archaeology Research Report 28.

Pavitt N. 1991, *Samburu*, London: Kyle Catrie Ltd.

Payne S. 1972a, 'On the interpretation of bone samples from archaeological sites', in *Papers in economic prehistory*, ed. E. S. Higgs, Cambridge: University Press, 65–81.

– 1972b, 'Partial recovery and sample bias: the results of some sieving experiments', in *Papers in economic prehistory*, ed. E. S. Higgs, Cambridge: University Press, 49–64.

– 1980, 'Animal bone report', in Lambrick G., Excavations in Park Street, Towcester, *Northamptonshire Archaeology* 15, 105–12.

Payne S. & Munson P. J. 1985, 'Ruby and how many squirrels? The destruction of bones by dogs', in Fieller et al. above, 31–40.

Pollard J. 1992, 'The sanctuary, Overton Hill, Wiltshire: a reexamination', *Proceedings of the Prehistoric Society* 58, 213–26.

Poplin F. 1975, 'La faune Danubienne d'armeau (Yonne, France); ses donnees sur l'activite humaine', in A. T. Clason (ed.) *Archaeozoological studies*, Amsterdam: New Holland, 179–92.

Potts R. 1988, *Early hominid activities at Olduvai*, New York: Aldine de Gruyter.

Rackham J. 1994, *Animal bones*, London: British Museum.

Rapson D. J. & Todd L. C. 1992, 'Conjoins, contemporaneity, and site structure: distributional analyses of the Bugas–Holding site', in Hofman and Enloe above, 238–63.

Rathje W. L. 1979, 'Modern material cultural studies', in *Advances in Archaeological Method and Theory* 2, 1–29.

Renfrew C. 1974, 'Space, Time and Polity', reprinted 1984 in *Approaches to social archaeology*, Edinburgh: University Press, 30–35.

Richards C. and Thomas J. 1984, 'Ritual activity and structured deposition in later Neolithic Wessex', in Bradley & Gardiner above, 189–218.

Ringrose T. J. 1993, 'Bone counts and statistics: a critique', *Journal of archaeological science* 20 (2), 121–57.

Robinson M. & Wilson R. 1987, 'A survey of environmental archaeology in the South Midlands', in *Environmental archaeology, a regional review 2*, ed. H. Keeley, Historic Buildings and Monuments Commission for England Occasional Paper 1, 16–100.

Ryder M. L. 1968, *Animal bones in archaeology*, Oxford: Blackwell Scientific Publications.

Sadler P. 1990, Report in Fairbrother J. R., *Faccombe, Netherton*, British Museum Occasional Paper 74 (2), 467–69.

Schiffer M. B. 1976, *Behavioral archaeology*, New York: Academic Press.

– 1980, 'Methodological issues in ethnoarchaeology', in Gould above, 29–47.

– 1983, 'Toward the identification of formation processes', *American Antiquity* 48, 675–706.

– 1987, *Formation processes of the archaeological record*, Albuqueque: University of New Mexico Press.

Serjeantson D. 1989, 'Animal remains and the tanning trade', with Waldron below, 129–46.

Serjeantson D. & Waldron T. 1989, *Diet and crafts in towns*, British Archaeological Report (British series) 199.

Shanks M. & Tilley C. 1987a, *Social theory and archaeology*, Oxford: Polity Press.

– 1987b, *Reconstructing archaeology*, London: Routledge.

Smith J. Z. 1992 (1987), *To take place: toward theory in ritual*, Chicago: University Press.

South S. 1977, *Method and theory in historical archaeology*, New York: Academic Press, 179–82.

Spurling B. & Hayden B. 1984, 'Ethnoarchaeology and intrasite spatial analysis: a case study from the Western Desert', in Hietala 1984a above, 224–40.

Stevenson, M. G. 1991, 'Beyond the formation of hearth-associated artifact assemblages', in Kroll & Price above 269–99.

Thomas J. 1990, 'Silent running: the ills of environmental archaeology', *Scottish Archaeological Review* 7, 2–7.

– 1991, *Rethinking the Neolithic*, Cambridge: University Press.

Thomas R., Robinson M., Barrett J. & Wilson R. 1986, 'A late Bronze Age riverside settlement at Wallingford, Oxfordshire', *Archaeological Journal* 143, 174–200.

Thorpe I. J. 1984, 'Ritual, power and ideology: a reconsideration of earlier Neolithic rituals in Wessex', in Bradley & Gardiner above, 41–60.

Voorrips A., Gifford D. P. & Ammerman A. J. 1978, 'Toward an evaluation of sampling strategies', in Cherry et al. above, 227–61 and Fig. 15.2.

Uerpmann, H.–P. 1976, 'Bemerkungen zur Aussagefahigkeit kleiner Tierknochen Fundkomplexe', in *Theme Specialise B Problemes Ethnographiques des Vestiges Osseux*, Nice: IX Congres U.I.S.P.P., 150–54.

Wade K. 1978, 'Sampling at Ipswich', in Cherry et al. above, 279–84.

Wainwright G. J. 1979, *Mount Pleasant, Dorset: excavations 1970–1971*, Report of the Research Committee of the Society of Antiquaries xxxvii.

Wainwright G. J. & Longworth I. H. 1971, *Durrington Walls: excavations 1966–1968*, Society of Antiquaries Report 29.

Wait G. A. 1985, *Ritual and religion in Iron Age Britain*, British Archaeological Report (British series) 149.

Whallon R. 1973, 'Spatial analysis of occupation areas', in *The explanation of cultural change*, ed. C. Renfrew, London: Duckworth, 115–30.

– 1984, Unconstrained clustering for the analysis of spatial distributions in archaeology', in Hietala 1984a above, 242–77.

Whimster R. 1981, *Burial practices in Iron Age Britain*, British Archaeological Report (British Series) 90.

Wilkinson M. R. 1985, in Lambrick above, 190–93.

Willis R. (ed.) 1994 (1990), *Signifying animals*, London: Routledge.

Wilson C. E. 1981, 'Burials within settlements in southern Britain during the Pre Roman Iron Age', *Bulletin of the Institute of Archaeology*, London, 18, 127–70.

Wilson R. 1975, 'Animal bones from the Broad Street and Old Gaol sites', *Oxoniensia* xl, 105–21.

– 1976, in Parrington M., 'Roman finds and animal bone from Kingston Hill Farm, Kingston Bagpuize,
Oxon.', *Oxoniensia* xli, 65–69.

– 1978a, 'Sampling bone densities at Mingies Ditch', in Cherry et al. above, 355–61.

– 1978b, in Parrington above, 110–39.

– 1979, in Lambrick & Robinson above, 128–33.

– 1980a, in Hinchliffe & Thomas above, 84–90.

– 1980b, in Palmer N., 'A beaker burial and medieval tenements in The Hamel, Oxford', *Oxoniensia* xlv, 198 and Fiche EO4–F11.

– 1984a, in Hassall et al. above, 265–68.

– 1984b, in Durham B., 'The Thames crossing at Oxford', *Oxoniensia* xli, 77.

– 1985, 'Degraded bones, feature type and spatial patterning on an Iron Age site', in Fieller et al. above, 81–94. Note that typesetting errors in the tables of this paper were not corrected after proof reading.

– 1986, in Miles above, Fiche VI.

– 1989a, 'Fresh and old table refuse', *Archaeozoologica* 3 (1.2), 237–60.

– 1989b, in Hassall et al. above, 258–68.

– 1989c, 'Trade, industrial and domestic activity at the old Clothing Factory, Abingdon', *Oxoniensia* liv, 279–86.

– 1990a, in Allen T. G. above, 94–106.

– 1990b, in Anon, 'Winsmore Lane, Abingdon', *CBA–9 Newsletter* 20, 90–93.

– 1992, 'Considerations for the identification of ritual deposits of animal bones in Iron Age pits', *International Journal of Osteoarchaeology* 2 (4), 341–49.

– 1993, in Allen & Robinson above, 123–45, 168–204 and 237–49.

– 1994, 'Projects modelling the spatial patterning of bones: limited success in publication', in Luff & Rowley-Conwy above, 57–66.

– 1995, 'On the curious distortions behind the charge of scientism against environmental archaeology', *Scottish Archaeological Review* 9/10, 67–70.

– Unpublished a, Mount Farm, Berinsfield, in Lambrick unpublished above.

– b, Bone report for Hardings Field, Chalgrove, in Page et al. unpublished above.

– c, Bone report for Wally Corner, Berinsfield, in D. Miles unpublished.

– d, Bone report for High Street sewer pipeline, Oxford, in Durham above.

– e, Bone report for St Michael Street, Oxford, in Durham above.

– f, Mapping the household activity of early Oxford, in Durham above.

– g, Bone report for The Causeway, Bicester, Oxfordshire, in Chambers R. in prep.

– h, Bone report for Misbourne Viaduct, Buckinghamshire., in Farley M. in prep.

– i, Middle Iron Age bone report for Lechlade, Miles & Palmer in prep. above.

– j, Bone report for the Vineyard III site, Abingdon.

Wilson R., Bramwell D. & Wheeler A. 1979, Reports in Parrington M., Excavations at Stert Street, Abingdon, *Oxoniensia* xliv, 16–23.

Wilson R. & Edwards P. 1993, 'Butchery of horse and dog at

the Witney Palace, Oxfordshire, and the knackering and feeding of meat to hounds during the Post–Medieval period', *Post–Medieval Archaeology*, 27, 43–56.

Wilson R., Grigson C. & Payne S. 1982, *Ageing and sexing of animal bones from archaeological sites*, British Archaeological Report (British series) 109.

Wilson R. & Levitan B. unpublished, Bone report for Late Iron Age and Romano–British site at Claydon Pike, in Miles & Palmer in prep. above.

Wilson R., Thomas R. & Wheeler A. 1979, 'Sampling a profile of town soil–accumulation', *Oxoniensia* xliv, 26–29.

Wilson R. & Wallis J. 1991, 'Prehistoric activity, Roman building and medieval tenements and gardens behind Twickenham House, Abingdon, *Oxoniensia* lvi, 1–16.

Woodward A. & Leach P. 1993, *The Uley shrines: excavation of a ritual complex on West Hill, Uley, Gloucestershire: 1978–79*, English Heritage Archaeological Report 17.

Wymer J. 1982, *The Palaeolithic age*, London: Croom Helm, 233–46.

Yellen J. E. 1977, *Archaeological approaches to the present*, London: Academic Press.

Yoffee N. & Sherratt A. (eds.) 1993, *Archaeological theory: who sets the agenda?* Cambridge: University Press.